ABBEVILLE PRESS
ENCYCLOPEDIA OF NATURAL SCIENCE

The World of Fish is one of the first four volumes in Abbeville Press's outstanding new collection of pocket encyclopedias of natural science. Written in scholarly yet easy-to-understand language, the series is packed with information that will fascinate student and nature buff alike. Beautiful full-color illustrations on every page supplement the lively text.

The World of Fish offers a comprehensive overview of the structure, locomotion, feeding, reproduction, behavior, habitat, and classification of fish. The volume combines the usefulness of a reference work with the readability of a browsing book, perfect for anyone attuned to the splendor of our natural world. It both explains and illustrates how fish breathe, what they eat, how they swim—and more.

Together with *The World of Birds, Insects,* and *Amphibians and Reptiles,* these books form the cornerstone of an indispensable home library—one that is almost guaranteed not to sit idly on the shelf.

The World of
FISH

BY FRANCO DE CARLI

TRANSLATED FROM THE ITALIAN BY Jean Richardson

ABBEVILLE PRESS • PUBLISHERS • NEW YORK

Library of Congress Cataloging in Publication Data

De Carli, Franco.
   THE WORLD OF FISH.

   (Abbeville Press encyclopedia of natural science)
   Translation of Il mondo dei pesci.
   Bibliography: p. 252-3
   1. Fishes. I. Title.
QL615.D313   597   79-1436
ISBN 0-89659-029-1 pbk.

Printed and bound in Italy by Officine Grafiche of Arnoldo
Mondadori Editore, Verona.

Contents

Introduction

Two and a half thousand million years ago, water appeared on Earth for the first time. It is hard to imagine a more catastrophic event. The water vapour that came out of the Earth's crust along with other gases accumulated in the primordial atmosphere, and formed a layer of cloud tens of kilometres thick that covered the sky. Condensation caused rain, but the temperature of the Earth's crust was so high that the fallen water at once re-evaporated. Then as the temperature slowly fell, the evaporation of the water lessened. The rain went on falling without stopping for hundreds of years. It was the greatest downpour ever, and when it stopped, more than three-quarters of the Earth's surface was covered with water.

The first life forms appeared in the oceans about two thousand million years ago and from this time water played a very important part in the evolution of living forms. Life began in the water; first algae and plants, then the invertebrates. The first ancestor of the vertebrates appeared perhaps as much as seven hundred million years ago. It was probably derived from a

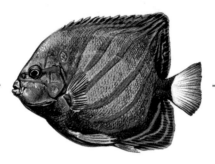

creature like the larval form of the echinoderms, and had the beginnings of a neural cord running through it and a hardening of the tissues surrounding it. This organ, the forerunner of the vertebral column, is known as a notochord, and animals that have one are called chordates. This includes fish, birds, reptiles, amphibians and mammals.

The aquatic vertebrates
One of the first chordates was *Ainiktozoon*, an animal whose head was fused to its body and whose vertebrae were rudimentary. This animal was probably the ancestor of the armour-plated 'fish' that appeared in the Ordovician Period. From it are derived not only all fishes today but also the other vertebrates, the amphibians, which in turn gave rise to reptiles, birds, and mammals. The first fishes probably developed even before the Ordovician Period, in the Cambrian Period, which was about six hundred million years ago. Living fishes today are totally different in appearance to these primitive fishes. Their life was

lived in a very different environment from that of today: the oceans were warm and not very deep, and they were populated by crustaceans, Protozoa and many forms of animal and vegetable plankton. Fishes moved in these surroundings at random, and were far from being the competent swimmers of our seas today. Their food consisted of tiny planktonic organisms or organic detritus in the mud on the bottom of the sea. This matter was sucked by the fish through its jawless, mouthlike opening.

The ostracoderms, the first fossil representatives of the armour-plated 'fish', were agnathans (without jaws) and their heads and part of their bodies were covered with bony plates. In modern times they have been divided into several groups, amongst which are the classes Cephalaspidomorphi and Pteraspidomorphi and the sub-class Thelodonti.

The cephalaspids are the best known ostracoderms. They lived in freshwater in the Silurian and lower Devonian Periods, and there were many species varying in length from a few centimetres to a metre. They had cephalic shields, pseudo-fins, and an asymmetric tail fin. A very interesting representative of this order was *Cephalaspis*, which led a very active life and was not confined to the bottom like the majority of fish of this period. The pteraspids and the thelodonts also lived in the seas and continental waters in the Silurian and Devonian Periods. They were usually flattened in shape and the tail fin was asymmetric and inverted, that is with the vertebral column ending in the lower lobe of the tail.

With the exception of the *Thelodus*, which was covered in tiny scales, all the vertebrates of this period were well covered in massive bony armour and some cephalaspids also had electric organs which were plainly defensive. What could have been a danger to vertebrates, however primitive, in a world inhabited solely by invertebrates? Probably the seas were inhabited by some giant arthropods, the Eurypterida, which appeared in the Cambrian Period and could both swim actively and crawl on the bottom. They vaguely resembled a cross between a scorpion and a shrimp, and the members of the genus *Pterygotus* were as much as three metres long. They were real monsters, and although slow in their movements could make trouble for even the most armoured primitive fishes. Fossils of these predatory invertebrates have been found alongside fossils of fishes of the same period, thus confirming their existence together and the danger they represented to the first vertebrates. At the end of the Devonian Period, 320 million years ago, more active fishes began to develop. Then the Eurypterida, unable to compete with these fishes began to disappear.

In the Devonian Period, contemporary with the ostracoderms, the representatives of the vertebrates with jaws (the super class Gnathostomata) increased. These were the placoderms, fishes without armour and with several anatomical innovations. As well as distinct jaws, they had well developed anterior as well as posterior fins. This enabled them to get away from their life of being confined to the bottom, and gave them a certain superiority over all other forms of life. The jaws offered new possibilities for catching food and permitted a more varied diet. At the same time the gills were modified and arranged in arches. It seems that the jaws may have developed from the first pair of gill arches, and not *vice versa*. This theory has been supported by the discovery of a primitive Elasmobranch, the *Cladoselache*. This was one of the cartilaginous fishes that appeared in the Devonian and from which it has been claimed, are derived the sharks and rays of today.

The Acanthodii, a group of placoderms, lived in between the Silurian and Permian Periods, or 350 to 200 million years ago. Small size vertebrates, they lived in freshwater and resembled sharks, so much so that they have been called spiny sharks. Their armour is made up entirely of tiny scales, very similar to the ganoid scales of the first bony fish, of which the Acanthodii are now thought to be the ancestors. The last acanthodians existed about 200 million years ago, in the lower Permian Period.

Bony fishes, in fact, appeared 300 million years ago, in the Devonian. One of the first typical examples, *Cheirolepis*, was an animal with very similar characteristics to modern fish. It looks quite modern with its large eyes, well developed mouth, paired pectoral and pelvic fins, and a dorsal fin opposite the anal fin. *Cheirolepis* belongs to the order Palaeoniscida, which includes fishes thought to be the ancestors of all the Actinopterygii, so called because of the presence of fins with rays. Other bony fishes, often classified together as the Sarcopterygii, adapted to life in freshwater, appeared in the Devonian, and comprise an important element of primitive fishes. They are subdivided into Crossopterygii (tassel-finned fishes) and Dipnoi (lung-fishes). The latter, without great modification, gave rise to the lung-fishes of today, while the crossopterygians started a new chapter in Earth's history.

The origin of land vertebrates

A typical primitive crossopterygian, *Osteolepis,* lived in freshwater and in the swamps of Europe and North America in the upper Devonian. Like the similar *Eusthenopteron*, it shows the first structural modifications that had taken place with the appearance of the tetrapods, the first land vertebrates. When the pools and swamps dried up, *Eusthenopteron* found itself in an advantageous position in relation to other fishes because it could breathe out of water, like the lung-fishes of today. In this environment, moreover, *Osteolepis* and *Eusthenopteron* probably had the capacity to move from one pool to another, unlike other fishes. The amphibians, the first land vertebrates, appeared in this kind of habitat about 250 million years ago.

9

▼ *Jaymoytius kerwoodi*

▼ *Mene rhombea*

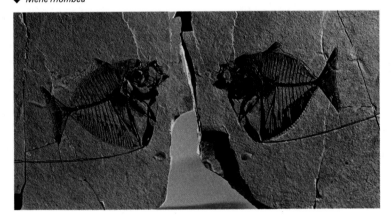

Fossil fishes

One of the oldest known fossil fishes is *Jaymoytius kerwoodi*.
This interesting example, found in the Silurian deposits of
Scotland together with *Ainiktozoon*, is actually an agnath and
similar to the ancestor of the cyclostomes (lampreys) of today.
Jaymoytius had a round mouth and symmetrical eyes and was
covered with rudimentary scales. It probably swam with the aid
of its assymetric tail and rudimentary swimming folds, like fins.

A fossil, *Palaeoniscus blainvillei*, of the order Palaeoniscida is
found in deposits at Autun in France. Some palaeontologists
suggest that the palaeoniscoids were derived from placoderms

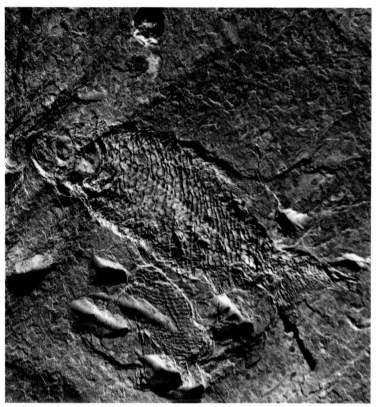

▲ *Palaeoniscus blainvillei*

like the genus *Acanthodes*. If one excludes *Acanthodes,* the palaeoniscoids are the oldest known bony fishes. They lived from the Devonian Period to the lower Cretaceous, and had a considerable variety of forms. The presence of fins with rays (Actinopterygii) and of ganoid scales was characteristic of this group. One of the largest deposits of fish fossils in the world exists in the Lessini mountains, at Bolca, near Verona. They go back to the Eocene Epoch, about sixty-five million years ago, and are of considerable variety. One of the best known fishes found at Bolca was the *Mene rhombea.* Fossils of reptiles, plants and insects have also come to light in the Bolca deposits.

▲ Bichir *Polypterus senegalus*

Living fossil fishes
Some representatives of these fishes from past epochs are still
living today. A group that includes 'living fossils' is the Dipnoi,
(the lung-fishes), with *Neoceratodus* in Australia, *Protopterus* in
Africa, and *Lepidosiren* in South America. These living
representatives differ from the primitive *Dipterus* only in
external appearance; they have retained the reduced gill
apparatus and also have lungs for breathing air. If the water is
well oxygenated *Neoceratodus* breathes through its gills, but it
uses its lungs when oxygen dissolved in the water becomes too
little. The *Protopterus* species, like their South American
relative, breathe only with their lungs; moreover if the
environment in which they live dries out, they can survive by
burying themselves in the lake or river mud. They can remain
in this state up to four years, waiting for water to return, most
of their body systems inactive and breathing through a hole in
their mud coccoon or tunnel.
    Another living fossil is the bichir, *Polypterus senegalus*,
representing the order *Polypteriformes*, that is known as fossils
from the Eocene but which probably originated in the
Cretaceous Period. Equipped with hard, shiny 'ganoid' scales
and a series of small dorsal finlets supported by spines, it lives
in the freshwaters of the great African rivers and lakes Chad
and Rudolph. The bichirs, like the lung-fishes, are able to
breathe oxygen from the atmosphere through a connection
between the throat and the swim-bladder, which was partly

▲ Common garpike *Lepisosteus osseus*

▼ Paddlefish *Polyodon spathula*

13

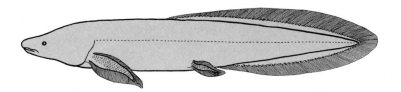

▲ Australian lung-fish *Neoceratodus forsteri*

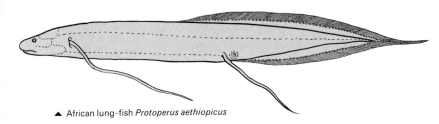

▲ African lung-fish *Protoperus aethiopicus*

transformed into a breathing organ. Other species of living fossils are the garpikes *Lepisosteus* and the paddlefish, *Polydon.* The former live in the freshwaters of North America and Mexico. The members of the family Polydontidae belong to the same order as the sturgeons, the Acipenseriformes, but they have a scaleless skin and a long snout like a spatula; two

▼ Shortnose gar *Lepisosteus platostomus*

species are known, one in North America, the other in China. The garpikes are covered with ganoid scales and have a slightly heterocercal caudal fin.

The coelacanth

Towards the end of the Palaeozoic the rhipidistian fishes became extinct. But a related group, the coelacanths, to which *Coelacanthus* belonged, survived. These fishes were thought to have become extinct at the end of the Cretaceous Period. But in December 1938, off the mouth of the River Chalumna in South Africa, a strange fish that had never been seen before was caught. It aroused the curiosity of the fishermen so much that they took it to Miss C. Latimer, of the East London Museum. The fish was clearly hitherto unknown, and the ichthyologist J. L. B. Smith of the University of Grahamstown was told of its capture. Although the fish was incomplete because it had been stuffed, Smith recognised it as a direct descendant of the coelacanths. Professor Smith distributed posters about the catch in the hope of getting another example, but it was not until December 1952 that another *Latimeria* was caught.

The living coelacanths are squat in appearance and more than a metre long, sometimes reaching a metre and a half. They weigh from 50 to 75 kilograms. The body is dark blue or brown in colour, slimy because of the presence of a large amount of mucus, and is covered with a particular type of scale, cosmoid, not found on any other species. Most of the fins are on short jointed limbs, with a wide range of movement. The heart is very simple. The intestine has a spiral valve. The vertebral column is rudimentary. The strong dorsal fin is supported by hollow cartilage that gives the whole group its name: coelacanth means 'with hollow spines'.

▼ Coelacanth *Latimeria chalumnae*

The 'watery planet'
The Earth is a sphere with a surface of just over 500 million
square kilometres. Dry land occupies only a small part of this
immense surface, in fact, it barely covers 30 per cent. Thus
Earth can be called the 'watery planet', not only because water
covers so large a part of it, but because life came from the
water. The Earth is the only planet in the solar system that has
water in a liquid form. It is also present on the other planets,
but in the form of ice or vapour, or imprisoned in minerals.
The Earth has water in a free form in its oceans, rivers, and
lakes. Inland waters are usually 'fresh' water, because of their
rather low salt content. In the sea the water is indeed 'salt', with
a salt average of about 35 parts per 1000 (about 35 grams of
salt a litre). In the sea, the most plentiful salt is sodium
chloride, that is, common cooking salt. There are also other
salts, such as iodine, sulphur, and carbon, but in small
quantities. Among the metals present are magnesium,
potassium, calcium and many others, all in small quantities. If
the Earth were completely spherical, without mountains or
depressions, it would be covered by about 1,330 million
kilometres of water to a depth of around 4,000 metres.

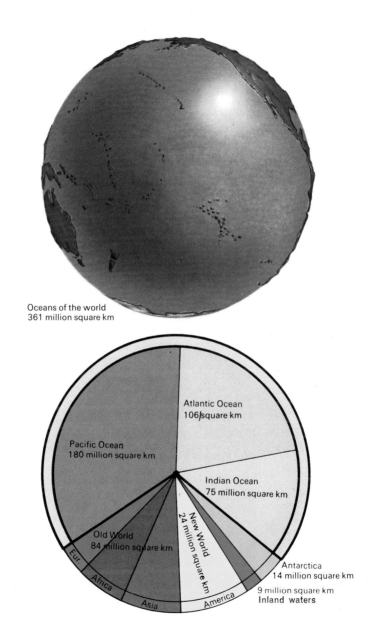

Oceans of the world
361 million square km

Pacific Ocean
180 million square km

Atlantic Ocean
106 million square km

Indian Ocean
75 million square km

Old World
84 million square km

New World
24 million square km

Eur

Africa

Asia

America

Antarctica
14 million square km

9 million square km
Inland waters

Life in the sea

The immense amount of space available to marine animals makes them the largest animal population on Earth. Fish are especially numerous. Shoals of herring calculated to contain more than two thousand million individuals have been seen. Herring shoals of this size are common although they are the subject of intensive fishing. It is probable that the seas of the world contain a weight of 500 million tons of fishes—and this total only takes account of those of certain food or commercial value. The living space of fishes varies from a depth of 11,000 metres in the Marianna Trench, in the Pacific Ocean, to a few centimetres of water in certain streams and on shores hardly touched by the sea. The extreme differences in the various aquatic environments permit fishes with a great variety of fantastic forms and sizes, from the tiny little Luzon goby, which is no more than a centimetre long when fully grown (lower right, a *Brachygobius nunus*, 4 cm long) to sharks like the *Rhincodon typus*, which is normally 14 metres long, but can be as much as 18 metres. The variety of sizes is matched by the considerable variety of colours—and the many colours of fishes are really fascinating. The fishes of some marine habitats, such as coral reefs, are incredibly beautiful.

▼ Bed of the Red Sea

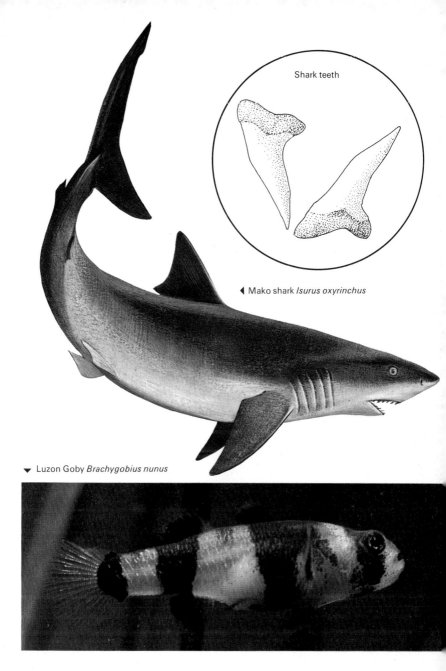

Shark teeth

◀ Mako shark *Isurus oxyrinchus*

▼ Luzon Goby *Brachygobius nunus*

Parallel with fishes, many other forms of life have developed in the water.

Invertebrates, which were present in the sea before fishes, are of immense importance, both in the food webs and in coral reefs, which are made up of the skeletons of countless individuals.

Sea urchins, sponges, and starfishes are among the best known sea invertebrates.

There is also a close relationship between aquatic invertebrates and some fishes. Some species live symbiotically with sea anenomes or jellyfishes which give them a home and safety. Invertebrates provide food for most fishes, but in the case of parasites they can also be the direct cause of death of many individuals.

Structure

Fishes today

Since their appearance fishes have been subject to the processes of evolution which, through natural selection, has profoundly changed their appearance. By eliminating the species least adapted to survive, natural selection has given fish complete dominion over the sea. The countless animal species that inhabited the water before the first fishes, and today still live in salt and freshwater, do not have the mobility and freedom to roam of fishes.

Convergence

Other vertebrates live in water and those that have succeeded

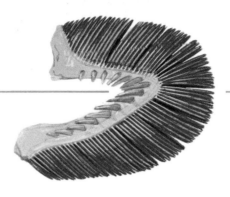

best demonstrate adaptations of body-form which make them resemble fishes, a phenomenon known as convergent evolution. Whales and dolphins are good examples of this kind of adaptation, which emphasises how the body shape of certain fishes may be the best available fit in relation to the environment in which they live. In fact the form of these cetaceans is modified so much that they resemble fish. Reptiles that lived in the Mesozoic epoch tried to adapt to an aquatic way of life and reached a stage of evolution similar to that of the modern dolphin. The Ichthyosaurs were good swimmers and had a vertical caudal fin like fish, whereas the cetaceans had a horizontal caudal fin. Ichychyosaurs became extinct about 70 million years ago. The enormous variety of fishes that exist has been determined by the vastness and variability of their environment. There are around twenty-five thousand species exhibiting an amazing variety of forms. The well-known seahorse is a fish in every way, despite its name and appearance. The box-fishes, the frog-fishes and the pipe-fishes, to which the seahorse is related, have an unusual appearance owing to adaptation to their surroundings. The hydrodynamic shape of the larger sharks is also the result of adaptation. For a predatory fish, such as the shark, the best solution is to have a body shape that permits the greatest possible speed. Every aquatic predator has a tapering body, because that is the shape most suited to their way of life.

Classification
Under the term 'superclass fish' zoologists class together animals with certain characteristics. That is to say that a fish, to merit the name, must have a skeleton equipped with vertebrae, a blood temperature equal to that of its surroundings, jaws, two nasal openings, and limbs in the shape of fins. This modern classification excludes from the superclass of fish the lampreys and the hagfishes, both usually thought of as fish.

The Agnatha
As we have just seen, lampreys and hagfishes are separate from other fishes because they lack some of the characteristics of that superclass. Lampreys and hagfishes lack jaws, which is why they are known as Agnatha (without jaws), as opposed to fishes, which are Gnathostomata. Moreover, unlike fish, they have only one nasal opening. They live in both salt and freshwater and some of them are fish parasites. The hagfishes sometimes attack fishes in difficulties, devouring their flesh and leaving the outer covering intact. Some lampreys attack live fish and do not abandon them until they die, feeding on the blood of their victims. The lamprey is responsible for a considerable diminution of local fish in the American Great Lakes. The Agnatha are descended from the ostracoderm fossils, that lived during the Silurian and Devonian Periods.

Cartilaginous and bony fishes
The superclass of fish has two classes: the Elasmobranchiomorphi, or cartilaginous fishes, and the Teleostomi, or bony fishes. The fundamental characteristic on which this subdivision is based is the constitution of the skeleton. Cartilaginous fishes have a skeleton made of cartilage, bony fishes are provided with a bony skeleton. This is not the only difference between the two classes, but it is the most important. A cartilaginous fish can have pronounced calcification of the skeleton, but never true bone, while a bony fish can have a partly decalcified or regressed skeleton, but will always have the basic bony structure. Other

systematic characteristics are the type of scales, the shape of the caudal fin, and the position of the mouth. Both cartilaginous and bony fishes are further divided into subclasses, orders, families, etc.

Morphology and anatomy of fishes

In both cartilaginous and bony fishes the head, the trunk, and the tail can be distinguished. The head is usually conical, and in bony fishes usually begins at the mouth opening (see diagram on p. 26, 1) and ends at the posterior edge of the gill cover (2). In cartilaginous fishes, the head begins at the snout (10), and the mouth is in a ventral position (1), and ends at the last gill opening (2). The trunk begins where the head ends, and the head is joined to the trunk in such a way that separate movement of the head is not possible. In the trunk are the digestive, excretory and reproductive organs, which are enclosed in a cavity called the coelom. In fishes the heart is outside the coelomic cavity and is inside the pericardial cavity. The opening of the anus, or cloaca, normally marks the end of the trunk. The trunk is followed by the tail, which has various shapes and is usually the propulsive organ of the fish. The fins, whose functions we shall see when dealing with movement, are the pectoral (again see diagrams on p. 26, 3), pelvic (4), anal (5), and dorsal (6); the asymmetrical type of caudal fin (7) is typical of the sharks, while in bony fishes it is usually symmetrical (7). Fishes have external eyes (9) and olfactory organs (8), and most cartilaginous fishes have a pair of spiracles (11). Some cartilaginous fishes such as the sharks and rays, and a few bony fishes such as the guppy and other killie fishes have external reproductive organs which in the cartilaginous fishes are modifications of the pelvic fins (12).

From the anatomical point of view we can distinguish in fish a skeleton, a muscular system, a circulatory system, digestive and excretory systems, a reproductive system, and a nervous system provided by the lateral line.

The external covering

Externally a fish is in touch with its surroundings through its epidermis, a covering of many-layered cells on top of a layer of connective tissue called the dermis. The epidermis houses many nerve endings and the organs of the lateral line. It is also equipped with numerous mucous glands that secrete the mucus which gives fishes their well-known slimy feel. Sometimes other types of glands which secrete venoms are also present. In certain deep-sea dwelling fishes the epidermis is equipped with luminous organs. The mucus from the mucus glands is of great importance in protecting the fish from bacterial infection and from attack by fungus or moulds. There is evidence that the slime on a fish's skin facilitates its passage through the water but an equally important function is to lubricate the sliding of the overlapping scales as the fish flexes its body while swimming.

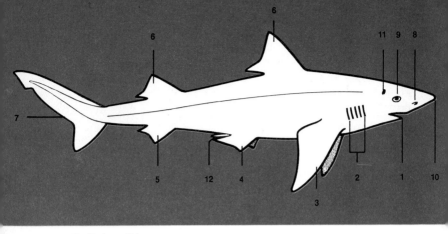

▲ Cartilaginous fish

The scales

The scales are hard skin formations that make up an external skeleton. The scales usually cover the whole animal, with the exception of the head and fins, but they can also be limited to one part of the body or distributed irregularly all over the fish. Scales are classified according to their shape and composition into placoid, ganoid, ctenoid, cycloid, and cosmoid (see diagrams on the right-hand page). Placoid scales are the most primitive type and are found only in Elasmobranchii, or cartilaginous fishes. They consist of a basal plate composed of dentine, and a tooth or spine, also of dentine and covered with enamel or vitro-dentine. The basal plate and part of the tooth

▼ Bony fish

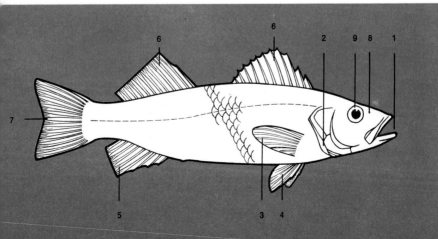

▲ Placoid scales   ▲ Ganoid scales

are hollow, and contain a pulp formed of cells called odontoblasts. The basal plate is buried in the dermis, but the tooth pierces the skin and emerges with its tip usually pointing backwards. The skin of sharks is like an abrasive covering of small teeth and, as shagreen, it was much used in cabinet-making and carpentry for polishing.

Ganoid scales owe their name to the fact that they are made of ganoine, a substance like enamel. They are four-sided, flat, and have the outside part equipped with minute teeth. These scales are typical of the palaeoniscoids in the Carboniferous and Permian Periods; today they are found on the bichirs and gar-pikes.

▼ Ctenoid scales   ▼ Cycloid scales

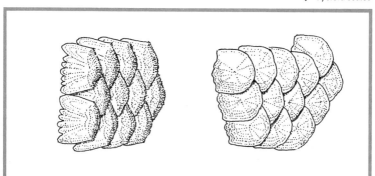

Ctenoid or cycloid scales are found on the majority of bony fishes. Fine, flexible and resistant, they do not have an enamel covering and are arranged like the tiles of a roof, so that one scale overlaps part of the next. They are placed in special pockets in the dermis, with the front edge in the pocket and the other at the surface and always pointing backwards. The scales are covered by the epidermis.

Coloration

Like their shape, colour is bound up with the daily life of fishes and performs a very important function. In the breeding season, for many species, it is one of the important elements of courtship. In some cases it is a means of recognition. The substances that produce the colours of fishes, that is the pigments, are found in the dermis and are grouped in chromatophores. These pigments are melanin, which produces a black colour, xanthin that makes a fish yellow, and erythrin that colours it red. Other pigments can also be found in the dermis or epidermis. Some colours, such as green and blue, are due to the phenomena of interference or refraction. The silver appearance of fish is due to crystals of guanin present in the dermis. There are also fish that are completely colourless or transparent, like the so-called glass catfish (*Kryptopterus bicirrhis*) and some centropomids.

◀ Comber *Serranus scriba*

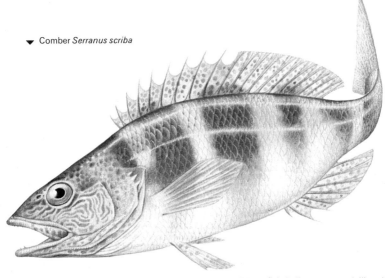

Triggerfish *Balistapus conspicillum* ▶

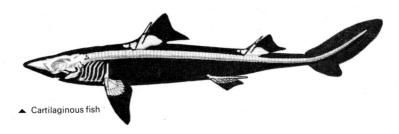

▲ Cartilaginous fish

The skeleton
The internal skeleton, or endoskeleton, is made up of various elements joined together by articulation. It can be subdivided into three parts: the head, the trunk, and the limbs. Bony fishes have a more complex skeleton than cartilaginous fishes and always have centres of obvious ossification.

The head
In both classes the head is made up of two parts: the neurocranium and the branchiocranium. The neurocranium is the part that surrounds and protects the brain case and the sense organ capsules; the branchiocranium, placed below it, includes the various parts of the skeleton concerned with the feeding and breathing functions of the fish. In cartilaginous fishes the neurocranium (A) is formed by cartilage that protects

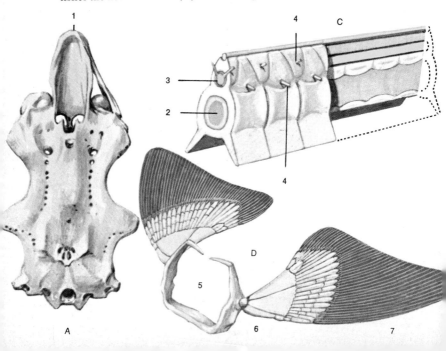

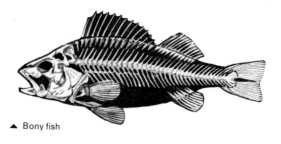

▲ Bony fish

on one side the brain and on the other capsules named after the regions they protect (optic, olfactory, otic). Often the neurocranium continues in front with the snout cartilage (1). In bony fishes, the neurocranium (B) is composed of numerous bones, joined together by sutures, articulations without mobility, and is considerably stronger than in cartilaginous fishes. The branchiocranium is made up of arches, which are, in order, the jaws or mandibular, jaw-support or hyal, and the gill or brachial arches. The mandibular arch forms the skeleton of the mouth and bears the jaw teeth. In cartilaginous fishes it is formed by the pterygoquadrate cartilage above and Meckel's cartilage below (the upper and lower jaws respectively). In bony fishes it is formed by the palatine, quadrate and pterygoid bones. In cartilaginous fishes the hyoid arch is formed by the hyoid and the hyomandibular.

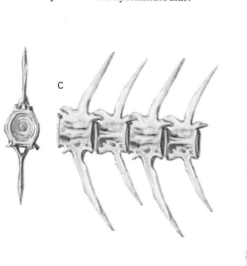

C

B

The trunk

The skeleton of the trunk, or axial skeleton, is formed by the vertebral column (see ill. C on pp. 30–31), which is made up of varying numbers of vertebrae. These form along the spinal cord (2) and are formed by the body of the centrum and the vertebral arches. There is movement between them and they have a cavity at each end. Inside the vertebral column is the spinal cord (3); this gives rise to the spinal nerves (4), that have the function of transmitting stimuli from various parts of the body to the brain and vice versa. Between the vertebrae—and especially in cartilaginous fishes—there are intravertebral bodies that facilitate the movement of the vertebral column during swimming, which, as we have already seen, is carried out in the majority of fishes by a waving movement of the tail and latter part of the trunk. In cartilaginous fishes there are also liquid-filled sacs that allows the transmission of movement without contact between the individual vertebral bodies. The vertebral arches are divided into the neural arches (dorsal) and the hemal arches (ventral). The neural arches join together to form the neurapophysis and the hemal arches form the hemapophysis. In bony fishes there are also ribs. The vertebral column ends in the tail, which has many varieties of shape.

The limbs

Like terrestrial vertebrates, fishes are equipped with limbs. Adapted for an aquatic life, these have the characteristic form of fins (D). But not all fins are derived from limbs. In other vertebrates limbs are equal, or in pairs, something that only applies to the pelvic and pectoral fins of fishes. As in other vertabrates, the limbs are provided with a shoulder girdle and a pelvic girdle. In bony fishes the girdles are made up of various segments, while they are simpler in cartilaginous fishes (5). They have some contact with the vertebral column, to which they may or may not be joined. The pectoral girdle joins the pectoral fins and the pelvic the pelvic fins. The outer part is called the free limb, and in fishes it is made up of basal skeletal parts to which the elements of the fins are attached. These are made up of rays of different kinds according to whether they are cartilaginous or bony fishes. In cartilaginous fishes, the fins are joined to the girdle by a formation of three basic pieces which carry the pterygiophores (6), on to which are grafted the ceratotrichia, or rays (7). These horny rays support the fin and are not usually visible from the outside because they are covered with a very thick epidermis. The ceratotrichia are translucent and flexible, and are made of elastic tissue and scleroprotein of a fibrous nature. They also occur in some bony fishes (such as salmonids) as support for the adipose fin. The fins of bony fishes also have pterygiophores, which are joined to girdles and carry the lepidotrichia, or bony rays. The fin membrane is usually translucent and the rays can be seen.

Biserial fins are characteristic of Dipnoi, *Latimeria* and many
fossil fish. They consist of an axial support that carries the
pterygiophores on opposite sides, into which the lepidotrichia
are inserted. They provide the lobed fins, endowed with great
mobility, that are thought to have been the ancestors of the
limbs of terrestrial vertebrates. The unpaired fins are of
vertebral origin, but hardly ever have any contact with the
vertebral column. They are supported by rays or
pterygiophores, sunk into the muscles or in contact with the
apophysis of the vertebrae. The unpaired fins also have
ceratotrichia or lepidotrichia, according to whether they are
cartilaginous or bony fishes.

The muscular system
The muscles of a fish account for from two-fifths to three-
quarters of its weight and are a vital part of its body. Fishes
such as tunnies and sharks are capable of considerable speed
and move in an environment about eight hundred times heavier
than air. This explains why their muscular system is rather
bulky. The muscle mass of a fish is subdivided into numerous
parts that form a very compact whole. The segments of this
muscular system are called myotomes, and the various
segments are closely related to the vertebrae. The myotomes
(see ill. on pp. 34–5, 1) are shaped like the capital letter sigma
of the Greek alphabet with the extremities turned towards the
plane running from the dorsal to the anal fin. They are divided
by two septa, one running through the aforementioned plane
and the other from side to side level with the vertebral column.
The latter plane divides the muscular system into hypoaxile (2)
and epiaxile (3). Each bundle of myotomes are further divided
by the myocommata (4). Fish also develop other muscles,
above all those responsible for the movement of the fins,
whether paired or unpaired. In some cases the unpaired fins
can be folded and therefore have an erecting muscle. Then
there are gill muscles, which are present in bony fishes to open
and close the opercula.

The digestive system
Depending on their life-style fishes eat a great variety of food
items, varying from that of the predator to that of the
plankton-feeder, from that of the detritus-feeder to that of fish
which are omnivorous. Each type of diet has a correspondingly
adapted mouth: pointed teeth, sometimes in several rows, for
predators like sharks; a complex filtering apparatus for
plankton-feeders; few teeth for the detritus-feeder; and all
purpose teeth for the omnivorous. Teeth can also be present in
the pharynx. After the oral cavity and the pharynx comes the
oesophagus (5) and the stomach (6). Besides helping with
digestion, the walls of this first part of the intestine are rich in
blood vessels and can have a respiratory function. One

33

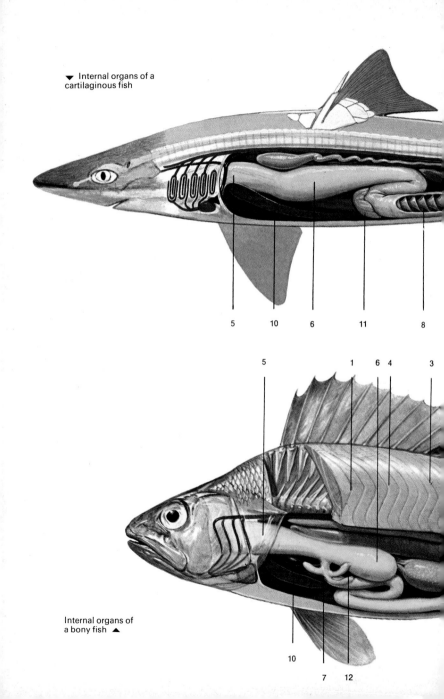

▼ Internal organs of a
cartilaginous fish

5   10   6   11   8

5   1 6 4   3

Internal organs of
a bony fish ▲

10

7   12

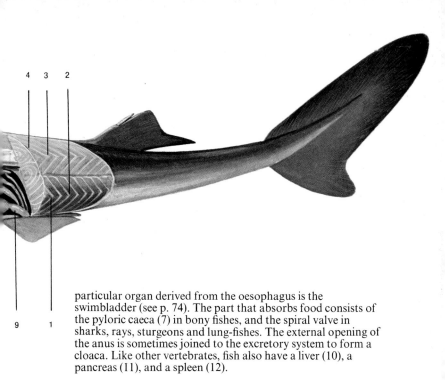

particular organ derived from the oesophagus is the swimbladder (see p. 74). The part that absorbs food consists of the pyloric caeca (7) in bony fishes, and the spiral valve in sharks, rays, sturgeons and lung-fishes. The external opening of the anus is sometimes joined to the excretory system to form a cloaca. Like other vertebrates, fish also have a liver (10), a pancreas (11), and a spleen (12).

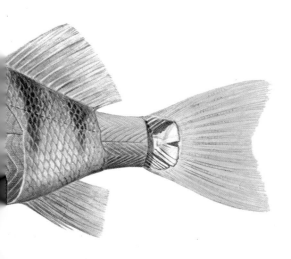

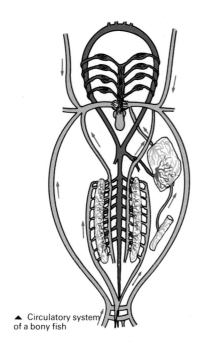

▲ Circulatory system
of a bony fish

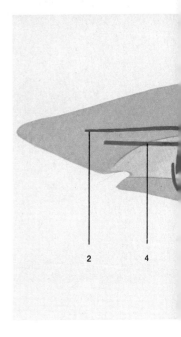

2   4

The circulatory system

Like amphibians and reptiles, fish are cold-blooded
vertebrates. As in other vertebrates, the blood is red because of
the presence of red corpuscles containing haemoglobin. It has
the important function of carrying oxygen from the gills to the
body and nutritive materials from the intestine to the organs
needing them. The circulatory system consists of the heart (1),
the arteries (in red), and the veins (in blue). There are some
differences in the hearts of cartilaginous and bony fishes. In the
selachians it consists of a sinus venosus, an atrium, a ventricle
and a conus arteriosus. In bony fishes the conus arteriosus is
reduced and has only a single valve, while in selachians there
are several. In bony fishes underneath the conus arteriosus
there is the bulbus arteriosus that continues into the aorta.
After being oxygenated in the gills, the blood runs through the
body in two large arteries: the carotid (2) towards the head and
the dorsal aorta (3) towards the tail. Parallel, but in the
opposite direction, run the anterior and posterior cardinal
veins (4), that meet in the common cardinal vein (5) to return to
the heart.

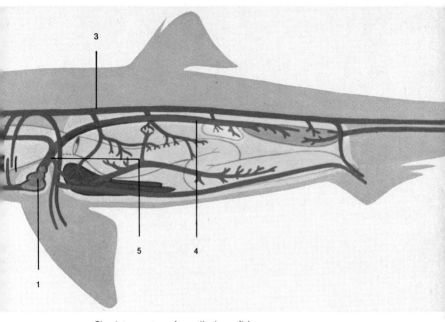

▲ Circulatory system of a cartilaginous fish

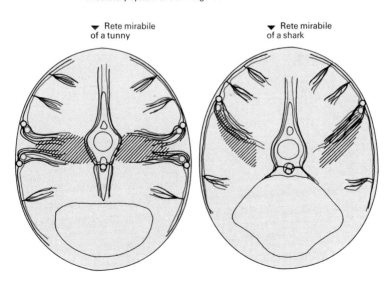

▼ Rete mirabile of a tunny

▼ Rete mirabile of a shark

The respiratory system

Unlike terrestrial animals, which take in oxygen from the air, fish use the oxygen dissolved in the water and give off the carbon dioxide they produce into the water. The set of organs in which these exchanges take place are the gills. Situated on either side of the pharynx are a series of arches which are part of the branchiocranium and which support the thin, richly vascularised plates of the gill filaments. The arches vary in number according to the species: usually there are five to seven in cartilaginous fishes and four in bony fishes, which may have fewer functional arches. Both the gills and the way of breathing vary in cartilaginous and bony fishes. In the fig. A below the breathing apparatus of a shark is illustrated, in B that of a bony fish. In the shark the water enters the mouth (1) and fills the oral cavity. Then the shark closes its mouth and reduces the oral cavity by contracting its throat. The water is thus forced out between the gill arches (2). Passing through the gill plates, it gives up oxygen to the numerous blood vessels whose thin walls permit the exchange of gases, at the same time absorbing the carbon dioxide given off by the blood which carries it from the body of the animal. The gills of all cartilaginous fishes communicate with their surroundings through the gill openings, which are clearly visible in the photograph alongside. In cartilaginous fishes, except for a few sharks and the Holocephali, there is a pair of spiracles (3) with pseudogills. Except in the rays these do not have a respiratory function, but seem to be an organ for regulating the blood pressure. In bony fishes (B) the water enters the mouth (1) while the gill covers (4) are closed. In a second the mouth closes and the oral cavity contracts, causing the water to be expelled through the gill opening, and passing over the gills (B, 5). In many bony fishes, the uptake of atmospheric oxygen is possible

◀ Gill slits of *Carcharhinus*

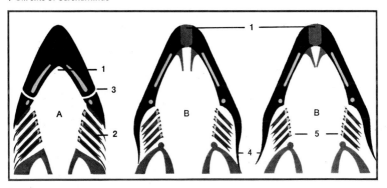

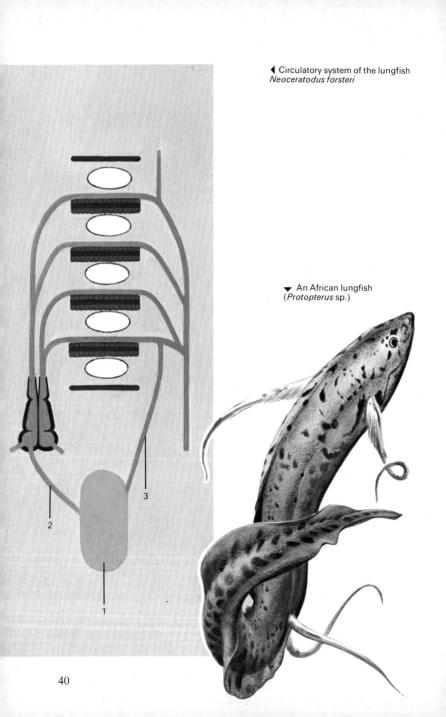

◀ Circulatory system of the lungfish
Neoceratodus forsteri

▼ An African lungfish
(*Protopterus* sp.)

40

through the skin, the walls of the mouth, the oesophagus, and the swimbladder. These organs are modified when they carry out respiratory functions. Usually they contain a network of blood vessels in the very thin walls, through which the exchange of gases is possible. The Australian lung-fish *Neoceratodus*, whose circulatory system is shown opposite, had a swimbladder (1) linked to the circulatory filaments of the pulmonary artery (3) and to the heart by the pulmonary vein (2). This fish of Australian rivers can, in unfavourable circumstances, breathe atmospheric oxygen through its swimbladder. *Protopterus*, which belongs to the same order, can stay in the mud during a dry season by breathing through a rudimentary lung. A South American freshwater fish, *Erythrinus*, uses gill respiration in well-oxygenated water; but if the level of the oxygen is low, or the water high in carbon dioxide, it breathes through its swimbladder, which resembles a lung. An African catfish of the genus *Clarias* has a branched organ, formed by a folded epithelium, that carries out the function of a lung. This organ is situated in a cavity above the gills, between the second and fourth gill arches.

▼ Air breathing organs

▼ *Protopterus dolloi*

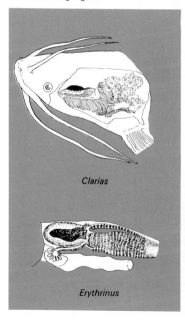

Clarias

Erythrinus

The 'internal' environment

Water is a fundamental component of tissues and is present in living organisms in quantities varying from 50 to 90 per cent. It constitutes about four-fifths of the total weight of fishes. Their life is therefore bound up with water and also with its salt content, which is found in their tissues, blood, and external environment. In order to explain the balance of life, it is necessary to explain the process of osmosis. Imagine a membrane that lets in water but at the same time prevents the passage of any salts dissolved in it: such a membrane is called semi-permeable. Now imagine putting this membrane in contact with two solutions, one, which we will call A, being more concentrated than the other, called B. Given that only water will be able to get through the membrane and that the two solutions will tend to reach the same concentration, the water in solution B will pass into solution A. This phenomenon is called osmosis. If we want to prevent the water passing from B to A, we will have to apply a certain pressure to solution A. This is called osmotic pressure. It depends on the concentration of salts in the solutions involved: the more concentrated solution A was, or the more diluted solution B, the higher the osmotic pressure would be. Almost all tissues behave like semi-permeable membranes, and the majority of vital processes are subject to the law of osmosis. It immediately becomes clear that the problems confronted by a fish are closely bound up with its surroundings and differ according to whether one is dealing with a marine or freshwater fish, or with a fish that lives

▼ Excretion in a freshwater fish

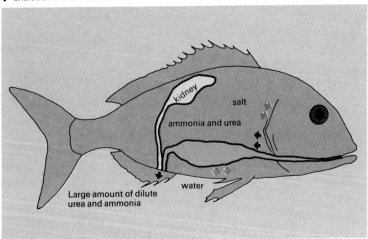

in brackish water, or with problems common to both marine and freshwater surroundings.

Now let us see how a bony fish behaves in freshwater. The surroundings are similar to solution B, while the fish's blood and tissues have a much higher saline content, like solution A. The freshwater that flows through the fish's gills so that it can breathe, passes by osmosis into its blood through the semi-permeable membrane of the walls of the capilliaries of the gills and of the mucus of the oral cavity. Thus the blood of a freshwater fish tends to become diluted, but for the fish to live, the concentration of the body fluids must not alter too much. It is therefore necessary to eliminate the excess water. The kidneys have the task of maintaining the concentration of the blood at the right level and also of eliminating in the urine the nitrogenous wastes produced by metabolism. This mechanism is not the only one to maintain the fish's body fluid equilibrium. It is also provided by the stomach, which enriches the blood with salt taken from food through the vessels surrounding the intestine. But equilibrium would not be reached without a further yield of salt, provided by the gills, which absorb salt from the water in a selective way, according to the needs of the fish. In salt water a bony fish is organised in a different way because its 'internal' saline content is lower than that of the surrounding water. Unlike what happens in freshwater, the marine fish tends to lose water through its gills and, to avoid becoming dehydrated, it must drink water. The salt water replaces the liquid lost, but introduces new,

▼ Excretion in a marine fish

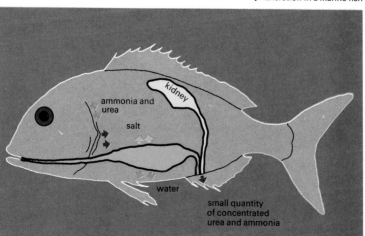

ammonia and urea

kidney

salt

water

small quantity of concentrated urea and ammonia

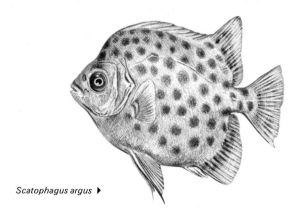

Scatophagus argus ▶

unneeded salt. The fish must eliminate it and does so through
its gills. It also expels with its faeces the salt brought in by food.
The kidney eliminate in the urine the ammoniacal salts and
small quantities of creatinine and uric acid. Cartilaginous fishes
have a special stratagem to prevent their blood from becoming
dehydrated: they produce urea instead of ammonia and avoid
expelling urine, thus increasing the concentration of their
blood to a slightly higher level than that of their external

▼ Grey mullet *Mugil cephalus*

surroundings. At the same time their kidney is fully functional. It is this peculiarity that has kept cartilaginous fishes in the sea, although some species live temporarily in freshwater, where the kidney eliminates a large amount of urine. It is interesting to note that in a day freshwater fishes eliminate urine the equivalent of about ten times their weight, as their body tissues tend to become diluted; in contrast, marine fishes eliminate very little urine, which is concentrated to avoid dehydration. In the urine fishes eliminate nitrogen in the form of ammoniacal salts, whereas amphibians and reptiles eliminate uric acid and mammals urea. All these processes take place in the kidney, which is joined to the reproductory apparatus. Fish have one kidney (1) called the mesonephros, and sometimes a pronephros (2) although this is usually atrophied; there may also be glands regulating the hydromineral exchange, and Stannius corpuscles in the mesonephros. The urine is carried by the mesonephric duct or ureter (3). The male reproductive system consists of a pair of testes (4), followed in cartilaginous fishes (A) by small coiled tube, a sperm duct and a seminal vesicle (6). In bony fishes (B) the testes (4) are followed by the mesonephric duct into the urogential papilla (5). Female cartilaginous fishes (C) usually have an ovary (7) connected to an oviduct, provided by a gland (8), to the uterus (9) and flowing with the deferent duct into the cloaca (10). In female bony fishes (D) the uterus (11) collects eggs from the ovary (7) and opens into the urogenital papilla (12).

▼ Urogenital systems of fishes

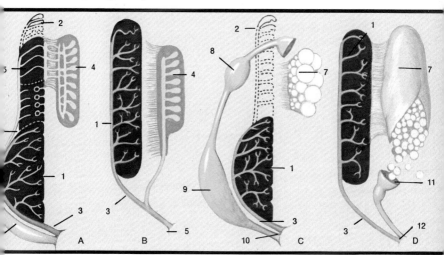

45

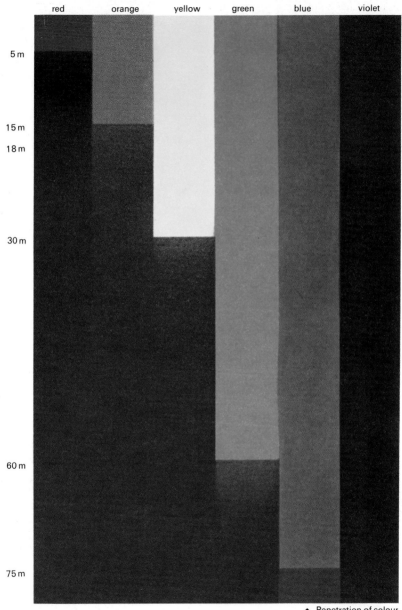

red   orange   yellow   green   blue   violet

5 m

15 m
18 m

30 m

60 m

75 m

▲ Penetration of colour
under water

46

Sight

As underwater divers know, the lack of visibility in water is one of the biggest difficulties to overcome. At depths of up to five metres, visibility is not very different from on the surface, but you only have to go down another couple of metres to notice the gradual disappearance of colours. At twenty metres a red fish looks almost black. The only distinguishable colours are yellow and violet-blue, which characterise the depths of the sea from twenty metres up to depths of a thousand or more metres, where the light disappears completely. The diagram opposite gives some idea of the colour penetration when the water is at its most transparent. Even a little plankton in the water can make it difficult to see more than a few metres beyond the end of one's nose, and very turbid water always resembles an impenetrable fog. In rivers there is almost total darkness at depths of only a few metres. But fish move with absolute mastery in these surroundings, so let us take a look at the structure of their eyes. The diagram below shows the typical eye of a fish which, unlike the eye of terrestrial vertebrates, focuses objects by moving the crystalline lens (1) without altering its shape. This movement is carried out by muscles (2). The eye has an iris (3). The sensitive layer is the retina (4), which has cones which are sensitive to colour stimuli and rods sensitive to light of varied intensity. There is a cornea (5), but its optical function is nil because it has the same refractive

▼ Section of the eye
of a bony fish

▼ Forward and
lateral vision

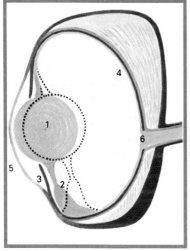

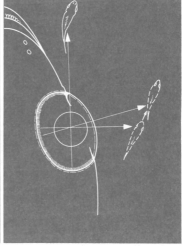

index as the medium in which fish lives. Fishes enjoy a wide
field of vision, but recent experiments have shown that their
sight is not as perfect as had been thought. They are in fact
long-sighted, and even more so when they are looking sideways
rather than in front, but this is an advantage rather than a
handicap. In fact, when they fix on prey in front of them, it is
framed in a field of vision in which they have the advantage of
both binocular vision and only minor defects of definition. At
the same time, the rest of their field of vision covers possible
movements rather than well-defined objects (see ill. on p. 47).
The stimuli are carried to the brain by the optic nerve (6) and
transmitted to the lobe on the opposite side from the eye,
accentuating the control of the lateral field of vision without
improving the binocular vision. Some sharks have a nictating
membrane, like an eyelid, which limits the amount of light that
reaches the eye when the fish moves from poorly-lit
surroundings to brighter ones, as when it rises from deep water
towards the surface. Those species which inhabit deeper water
often have larger eyes than their shallow-water relatives.
Species which live at depths of 200 to 1,000 metres have well
developed eyes with a retina which is extra rich in rods. The
eyes of the two moderately deep water fishes opposite are a
good example of organs adapted to their surroundings. The
large eyes enable them to make the most of the very weak
sunlight that penetrates to a thousand metres and to use the
pale light emitted by the numerous organisms that live at such
depth. In even deeper water the eyes of fishes tend to grow
smaller and may become atrophied.

▼ Binocular vision

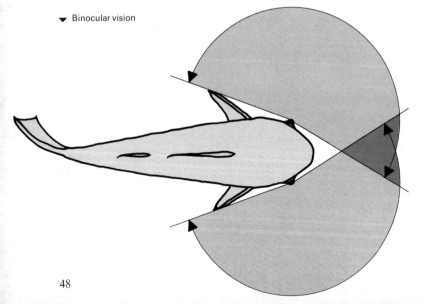

Smell

Drop a little blood in water where there are sharks and in a
short time all those within a radius of a few hundred metres will
be visibly agitated. Sharks are famous for appearing on the
scene whenever another fish is in difficulty, and this is mainly
because of their sense of smell. The hammerhead shark, like
other sharks, has two olfactory holes, or nostrils, with the
difference that they are situated on either side of the 'hammer'.
When this shark picks up a smell, it moves along a track in a
zig-zag fashion trying to find the right direction with its sense
of smell. If one of the shark's nostrils is blocked up, it will move
in a circle, because one nostril alone is not enough to direct it
towards the source of the smell. Sharks probably veer in the
direction of the nostril that receives the strongest stimuli. In

▼ Hammerhead shark *Sphyrna zygaena*

▼ Blue shark *Carcharius glaucus*

bony fishes the olfactory organ usually consists of two nasal capsules equipped, in most cases, with two openings. While the olfactory organs are well developed in cartilaginous fishes, in bony fishes they vary from the eel, which has a 'good nose', to the pike and the needle-fish, two predators incapable of picking out their prey unless it passes before their eyes. The morays, which are nocturnal predators, depend considerably on their sense of smell to find their prey. Their olfactory apparatus is shown below. The nasal capsules communicate with the outside world through two tubes which can be seen on the snout, above the mouth. The tubes (1) carry the water to the nasal capsules (2), which are lined with a folded epithelium, that constitutes the sensitive part and is linked by nerves to the brain. The water comes out of two holes (3).

▼ The Moray eel and its olfactory apparatus

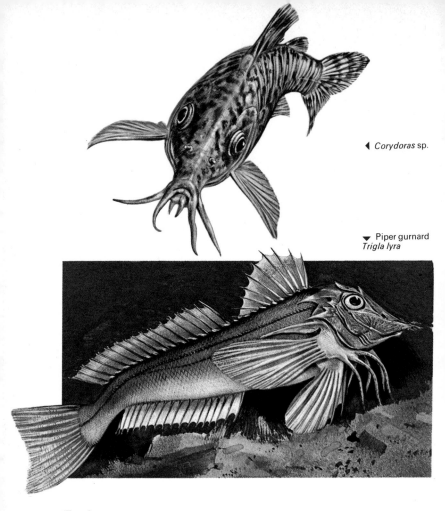

◀ *Corydoras* sp.

▼ Piper gurnard
Trigla lyra

Touch

If you watch a catfish in an aquarium, you get the feeling that they touch things with their barbels in order to find out where they are. But the barbels of catfish, and of fish in general, are really more like organs of touch than a cat's vibrissae, and have nerve endings that are sensitive not only to touch but also to vibrations and changes of temperature. One source of tactile sensation is the skin, which is rich in free nerve endings. Above all in fish in constant contact with the bottom, such as benthonic fishes, the sense of touch is very important in the search for food, which usually consists of detritus or crustaceans. In soles and other flat fishes, the unpigmented skin of the lower side is very important in the animal's choice of terrain. The ventral sucker of certain fish (gobies) has also a tactile function.

Taste
Watching a sturgeon swim lazily along the bottom, one cannot help wondering at the way it finds the tiny fish, molluscs and crustaceans it eats. The barbels in front of its protrusible mouth 'warn' it that they are in contact with food and the sturgeon hurriedly swallows it. The thoroughness with which these barbels perform their task makes one think that the sturgeon actually 'tastes' its prey in this way. The red mullet's barbels work in the same way. Grey mullet have taste buds on their body.

▼ N. American catfish *Ictalurus melas*

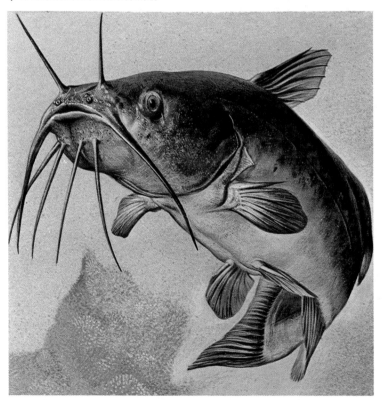

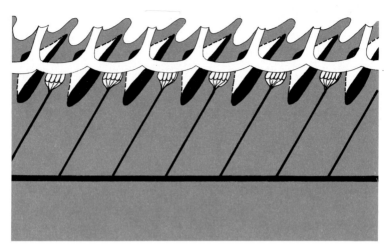

▲ Section through the lateral line

◢ Mediterranean parrot fish
(*Sparisoma cretense*) with
its prominent lateral line

The lateral line

In the water vibrations are diffused far more quickly than in the air, so it is logical enough that in order to move more efficiently in their surroundings fish have developed sense organs sensitive to vibrations. This sixth sense of fishes is called the lateral line, and it is so efficient that it makes the presence of eyes and barbels almost unnecessary. The lateral line is usually sited under the epidermis, along the flanks of the animal, and from the outside it looks like a different coloured stripe running from head to tail (see ill. opposite). Lateral line organs are also scattered on the head in many species. As seen in the diagram, the lateral line is formed by canals full of mucus that communicate with the outside world. In the canals are sense organs called neuromasts, and in normal conditions these send signals, which are always on the same frequency, to the fish's brain. But when the pressure on the neuromasts varies, the signals transmitted undergo variations of frequency and intensity, thus giving the fish a fairly complete picture of what is going on round about. The neuromasts are linked by nerve fibres to the central nervous system, which interprets the information supplied by more neuromasts and can thus determine the direction, intensity, and speed of the source of the vibrations. Vibrations with a frequency of twenty–thirty cycles a second, such as those produced by a struggling, harpooned fish, can attract dogfish within a radius of 250 metres. Many serious attacks by sharks happen to swimmers on the surface. Unlike a diver, who moves without making a noise, the surface swimmer strikes the water rhythmically like a fish in difficulty, thus attracting predators.

The functions of the lateral line are not limited to the predator-prey relationship and vice versa: it also serves the fish as a highly efficient short-range radar. A fish using sight alone would be unable to distinguish the glass walls of an aquarium: it is the lateral line that warns it of the obstacle, immediately detecting the object by alteration to the wave of water that the fish pushes in front of itself while swimming, which is known as the wave of compression. Seeing a salmon jump rapids on its return migration makes one think it must be very strong. In reality it makes use of its lateral line to take advantage of the currents created by the rapids. If possible, the salmon swims near the bottom or sides of the river where the current is less fast. When it rests, it always does so behind a rock or in a hole, where the water is almost still. When it has to jump out of the water to overcome a rapid, it almost certainly makes use of the ebb flow to give itself a boost. Thus it is clear that the lateral line is able to detect the slightest movements of the water, whatever they are like, so making the fish's movement easier even in turbid water where there is less visibility. Skin-divers say that the lateral line may also detect the intentions of that predator, man. Fish will usually come near a diver without weapons, but they run to take cover at the appearance of a diver with a gun, whose warlike intentions are as clear to the lateral line as those of any other predator.

Hearing

In fish the lateral line and the hearing organ share the same source. As in other vertebrates, this is the inner ear and the balance organ, or labyrinth. The ears consist of two capsules placed on the sides of the cranium, behind the eyes. Each capsule has three auditory chambers: the utriculus, the sacculus, and the lagena. The sacculus and the lagena are the seat of the auditory function. When the vibrations caused by sounds reach the fish's ears, they spread through these two chambers, where there are sensitive areas of ciliary cells that convey stimuli to the brain via the auditory nerve. The utriculus, situated above the sacculus and the lagena, has semi-circular canals that make up the labyrinth. There are two semi-circular canals on a vertical plane and one in a horizontal plane. At the end of each are swellings, or ampullae, equipped with a covering of ciliary sensory cells and crowned by a gelatinous dome. The system formed by the utriculus, the semi-circular canals and the ampullae contains a liquid called endolymph and some calcareous bodies, the otoliths. The static organ is so-called because it governs the balance of the fish, whose movements produce different movements of the otoliths

▼ Carp and the Weberian apparatus

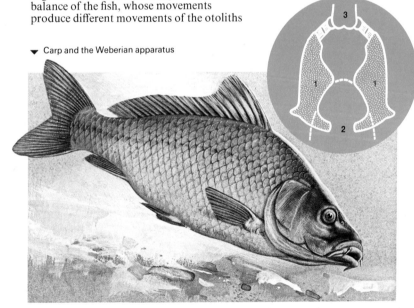

56

and the gelatinous dome. The ciliary cells readjust to the movements of the otoliths and the gelatinous dome by sending signals to the central nervous system. Also in turbid water, where there is not enough light to distinguish the top from the bottom and there are no points of reference for following a precise course, the fish always knows how to stay on course on the basis of signals provided by the labyrinth. The labyrinth also helps the fish to stabilise its field of vision. Living in surroundings that can be subject to strong turbulence, the eye can find it difficult to centre the image and keep it within its field of vision. The central nervous system moves the motor muscles of the eye according to signals received from the labyrinth; if the fish turns its head to the right, its eyes turn left, and vice versa. Even while swimming and in rough water the animal is thus able to fix an object in its vision.

The Weberian apparatus
Experiments carried out on minnows have shown that these tiny fishes from European rivers are sensitive to minute variations of pressure. The minnow, and other members of the order Cypriniformes have the Weberian apparatus, which consists of two little bones (ossicles) (1) that put the swim-bladder (2) in touch with the ears (3). The changes of pressure are transmitted to the swim-bladder and are conveyed to the labyrinth area by the Weberian ossicles, where they are translated into impulses that are sent to the brain.

▼ Connexion between the swimbladder and the inner ear in the carp family

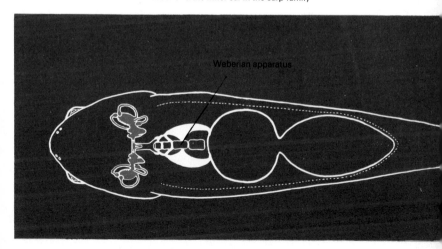

Movement

Movement in the water

Movement in a liquid is conditioned in the first place by the resistance of the medium, which is eight hundred times greater than the air. Anyone who has tried to run in water or to move an object in liquid surroundings knows how tiring it is. The same difficulty occurs if you want to immerse a flat object quickly: it is easier to do so from the side opposite to the direction wanted. And if the speed of these movements is increased, the difficulty and force needed become much greater. Fish are tied to this world and their movement is inseparably bound up with these problems. But time and evolution have helped the inhabitants of the waters to reach a satisfactory solution.

The study of hydrodynamics is a fairly recent subject for man. But in nature it could be said that it was undertaken when the first fish appeared, and that, when faced with his first hydrodynamic problems, man copied fishes. The streamlined shape of fish and their way of moving allows the maximum efficiency with the minimum effort; moreover, the solutions to the problem of movement are bound up with the lives and habits of the different species.

The various shapes of fishes are closely related to their habits and feeding requirements. An active or predatory fish has the form and means to swim quickly; a fish whose diet is composed of crustaceans and other animals that live on the bottom does not have a streamlined shape because it does not have to solve problems of speed, and its swimming organs are adapted so that it can move slowly in search of food. The different approach adopted by two fishes who feed in the same way—the herring and the frogfish—is significant. The first devotes its life to the constant search for plankton and swims tirelessly; the second attracts small animals to its mouth while remaining motionless on the bottom. Because of its active life, the herring's body has a streamlined shape that is totally different to that of the frog fish. Notice also the similarity in hydrodynamic shape between the tunny and the open sea sharks. The first is a bony fish, the second a cartilaginous fish, but both are predators and have evolved a shape well suited to top speeds of more than fifty kilometres an hour.

There are very few species of fish as fast as tunnies and sharks, but the majority have very similar shapes. The shapes resemble the spindles used by spinners, which is why these animals are called spindle-shaped fish. From the first appearance of fish the spindle shape has played a leading role, and many shapes created by evolution can be regarded as variations on this theme. The fishes of a coral reef give a clear picture of these variations: from the angel-fish with its laterally compressed body to eel-shaped fishes such as the morays, with a very long body. As for fishes which live on sandy bottoms, they tend to have a depressed body and very muscular fins that are more like wings than fins.

The movement of fishes

All fish can move in water, but they do not all move in the same way. Their shape is important for swimming purposes but their internal structure is even more important. It is this that limits them to particular movements. If you watch a fish swimming slowly, you can tell from its quick, sudden movements, that may seem the same to the human eye, whether it is a goldfish, a herring or a cod. It is useful to have a cinecamera to record the movements of fishes so that you can watch their swimming in slow motion. Two important observations can be made: the main part of the movement is not carried out by the fins but by the tail and latter part of the body; the movement is the result of a series of rhythmical flexures of the body. Analysing these flexures further, we see that they are made up of waves running along the body. The extent of these waves increases little by little until they reach as far as the head and the tail. The 'motor' that makes the fish swim is the series of muscular segments on either side of the vertebral column. These muscular segments, or mytomes, are an important part of a fish's body. An inactive fish, such as the well-known goldfish, has muscle equal to two-fifths of its total weight. A tunny, on the other hand, can have three-quarters of its weight made up of muscle. The myotomes are in close contact with the vertebral column and placed in such a way as to exercise their force by pulling crosswise on the joints that separate the vertebrae. The myotomes are also placed as if they were embedded in each other and usually slope from head to tail. This results in the flexure of the fish's body from one part to the other, according to whether the right or left side of the muscles is contracted. Swimming is thus an alternate contraction or distension of the fish's muscles. It is obvious that when the myotomes on the right side contract, those on the left side distend.

Fish also need to manoeuvre in their surroundings, to be able to perform turns and stops, and to make certain movements in reverse. These are carried out by other fins. If you watch goldfish in an aquarium, it is easy to surprise them carrying out little movements forwards, backwards and sideways, near the walls of the tank or some other obstacle. These fishes reveal considerable ability for manoeuvring: their pectoral fins are the most efficient instruments. These fins are most important to the stickleback (see p. 126) in the mating season. This little freshwater fish builds a nest where his mate will lay her eggs. The nest is made of plants joined together by a viscous secretion from his kidney. The stickleback uses its mouth in the building, but it could not do this without its pectoral fins. After the eggs have been fertilised the fins are used as a fan to create a current of water that keeps the eggs well-oxygenated. The unpaired fins, such as the dorsal and the anal, act as rudders and are also used to prevent vertical oscillations. Many species equipped with particularly well-developed dorsal fins can fold them back until they disappear, so that they can reach higher speeds in rapid swimming.

Swimming styles
We have seen how the flexing movement impels the fish; now let us look at the way the waves of flexure spread out in the water, producing the forward impetus necessary for swimming. By analysing the movements of various species in slow motion, we can see their different ways of swimming. It varies from the style of the tunny (see p. 62, 1), in which only the caudal fin moves, to that of the mackerel (2) and the shark (3), which displays the waves of flexion far more, and to the style of the eel, in which the waves convulse the whole animal (4). Both the eel and the tunny move in their surroundings without any difficulty, but the eel has virtually no caudal fin while the tunny has a very well developed one. To understand how different types of fish move, we must analyse the forces that create the movement. The undulations of the eel-shaped body (see p. 68, above) produce a series of movements in the water which are obliquely directed to both sides of the fish's rear.

This oblique movement can be divided into two components, one perpendicular to the fish and the other directed to the rear; the perpendicular forces cancel each other out, because those on one side compensate those on the other, but the rearward force makes the fish go forward. The swimming of spindle-shaped fishes is not very different: they reduce the oscillations of the body, but the impetus is supplied equally by the rear part and the caudal fin. If we watch the oscillating movement of the caudal fin, we shall see that the force it exerts on the water is directly oblique to the rear and, as in the case of the eel, can be divided into two parts. The tail and the body contribute to the movement to a different extent: in the eel it is only the body, in the tunny only the tail. We know that the tunny is one of the fastest fish, while the eel is rather slow in its movements.

It is obvious that the caudal fin makes the most important contribution to fast swimming. A special swimming style is adopted by the rays and the devil-rays or manta-rays, which are propelled by the impetus they receive from large pectoral

▼ Swimming movements of fishes   Swimming of a ray ▶

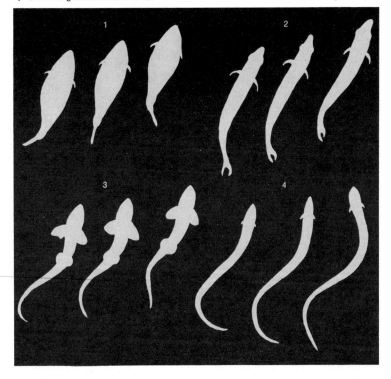

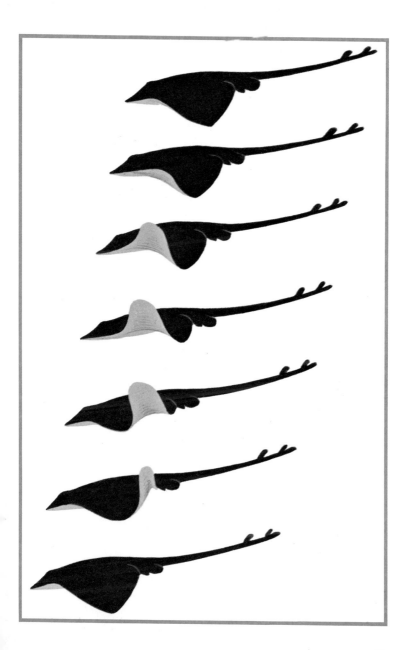

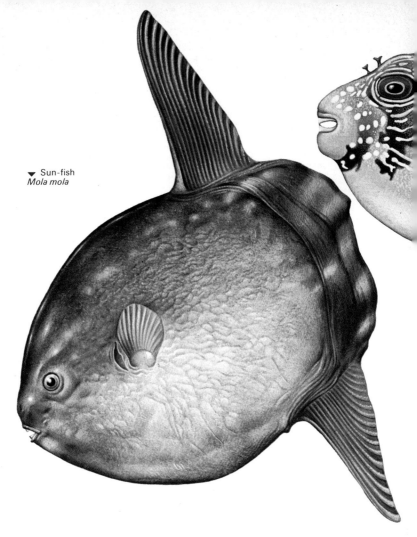

Sun-fish
Mola mola

fins which are like great wings. The rays are equipped with a
series of pectoral muscles that move the corresponding radial
cartilages, and they are perfectly suited to the sedentary life
they lead. The rays spend most of their time stretched out on
the bottom, and feed on tiny crustaceans or molluscs. Their flat
body is adapted to this life-style and allows them to disguise
themselves by covering themselves with sand flung up by their
pectoral fins. The manta-rays, which lead a more active life,
can jump right out of the water. The pectoral movement of
both the rays and the manta-rays reflects the typical movement

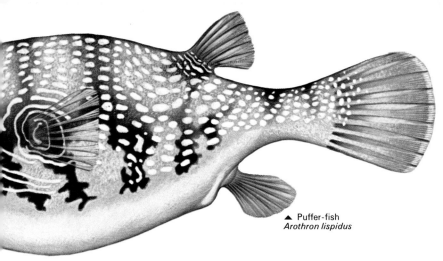

▲ Puffer-fish
Arothron lispidus

by waves of flexion that characterises the majority of fishes.
The sun-fish (*Mola mola*) is a cosmopolitan fish. It also lives in
the Mediterranean and can reach exceptional dimensions, with
a height of more than three metres and a weight of almost a
ton. This giant swims with its anal and dorsal fins, which are
opposite each other and very high. The sun-fish's caudal fin has
become atrophied.

The puffer-fish (*Arothron hispidus*) swims with its pectoral
fins aided by its dorsal and anal fins. The caudal fin acts just as
a rudder. The puffer-fish swims slowly, but it can protect itself

▼ Triggerfish *Balistes carolinensis*

by taking in water so as to increase its size greatly. The trigger-fish (*Balistes carolinensis*) moves like the puffer-fish, using its anal and dorsal fins. It also has a characteristic, spiky dorsal fin that it can erect when it likes but which plays no part in swimming. Surgeon-fishes (Acanthuridae) move by using their pectoral fins like oars. The trunk or box-fishes (Ostraciontidae) are literally enclosed in a rigid, bony box that prevents any movement of the body except for the tail, although pectoral, anal and dorsal fins move. The strangest of all fishes is perhaps the seahorse (*Hippocampus*), which moves by quickly vibrating the dorsal and pectoral fins. Its movement is slow, but adapted to the life it leads, usually attached to algae by its prehensile tail.

▼ Bonito *Sarda sarda*

Fast fishes

Best known in America, deep-sea fishing is carried out with a rod and fishing-line on board boats built for this purpose that cruise slowly in fishing areas. The fishermen hope to catch pelagic fish such as sharks, tunnies and bonitos. Once hooked, these fish fight actively and swim fast, and by measuring the amount of line they draw out in a given period of time, it is possible to work out the speed at which they make off. The wahoo (*Acanthocybium*), a relation of the tunny, is just under two metres long, but when in flight it pulls out the first hundred

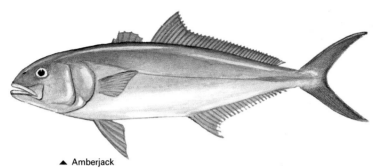

▲ Amberjack

metres of line at a speed of more than 65 km an hour. Sharks too are subject to intensive deep-sea fishing. Their speed is plainly slower, but even they can maintain 40 km an hour. All the speed records are held by fishes with a crescent-shaped tail. Considering tunnies, sharks, bonitos, and amberjacks, we can see an obvious similarity in the shape of the caudal fin. Plainly evolution has caused very different species to adopt the most efficient form of propulsion. All these fast fish use a swimming style based almost exclusively on caudal propulsion and do not depend upon the waves of flexure along the body. The founder of this school is the tunny (*Thunnus thynnus*), which reaches a maximum speed of more than 70 km an hour. Its tail is more

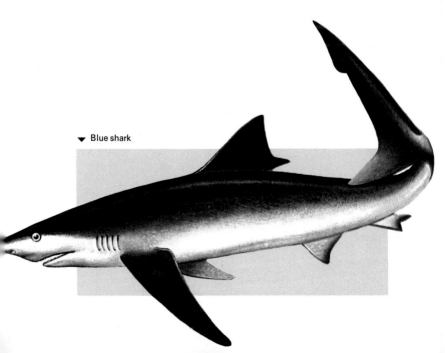

▼ Blue shark

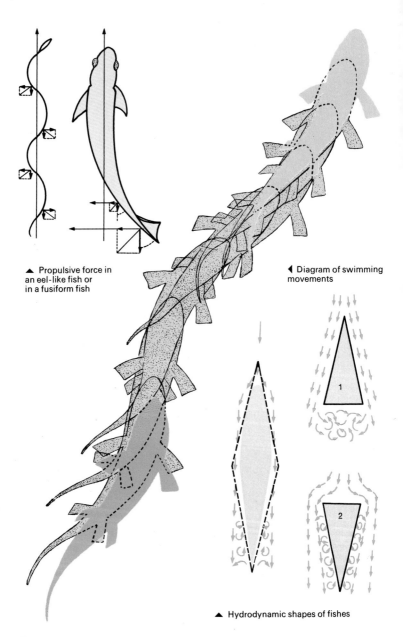

▲ Propulsive force in an eel-like fish or in a fusiform fish

◀ Diagram of swimming movements

▲ Hydrodynamic shapes of fishes

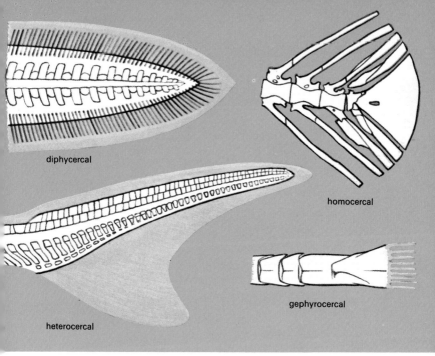

diphycercal

homocercal

heterocercal

gephyrocercal

▲ Types of caudal fin

like an aeroplane propellor than a swimming organ, and like an aeroplane without a propellor, the tunny is incapable of the smallest movement if deprived of its tail.

Tails differ in their morphology, which often reflects a distinctive internal structure. They are subdivided, on the basis of how the vertebral column ends, into types known as diphycercal, heterocercal, hemocercal, and gephyrocercal. The diphycercal tail fin is typical of eels and is characterised by complete symmetry between the dorsal and ventral parts. This kind of tail can also be seen in many fish embryos. Sharks have heterocercal tails, characterised by an asymmetry that, in the case of the thresher shark, is considerable, with the longer lobe of the tail reaching a length of around two metres. Heterocercal tails have a characteristic feature, linked to the particular structure of the two caudal lobes, of which the lower is far more flexible. The vertebral column continues into the tail as far as the apex of the upper lobe. The sturgeon and all the other Acipenseriformes have heterocercal tails. The majority of bony fishes have homocercal tails that seem to be symmetrical. But by analysing the structure of the bony parts of the tail, we can see the asymmetry of the vertebral column. Angler fishes and

▲ Spearfish

many other benthonic fishes have a gephyrocercal tail, which is very reduced. The tails that do the most to increase speed are the homocercal and the heterocercal, which have the greatest elongation (that is, the relation between the height of the tail and its surfaces). There is, however, another element that has not been dealt with: the resistance met when swimming is connected with the shape of the fish, and this can be an important factor in limiting speed. The spindle-shape of the fastest fishes is the best from the hydrodynamic point of view. It is similar, in the main, to that of two cones joined at the base (see p. 68 below). The front part (cone 1) of this model has good penetration and an absence, or almost, of turbulence in the tail region (cone 2). It should be pointed out, however, that speed depends more on the caudal fin than on the shape of the head. If we compare two very fast fishes, such as the tunny and the swordfish, we notice that the rear of the body is an almost identical shape, unlike the front part where the swordfish carries its 'sword'. The same is true of the marlin (*Makaira*), which has a shorter snout than the swordfish but it is just as fast.

Swordfish ▶

▼ Pike
Esox lucius

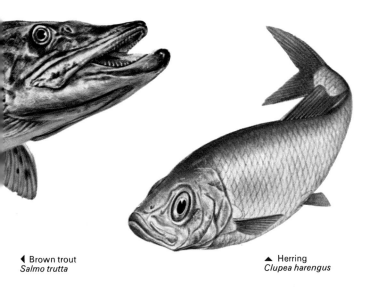

◀ Brown trout
Salmo trutta

▲ Herring
Clupea harengus

Speed and resistance

We have seen that the fastest fish are those with tapering bodies
and a considerable amount of muscle, but to function the
muscles need fuel and combustion like any motor. In
vertebrates the 'fuel' is provided by the food which is taken in
and absorbed by the blood, mainly in the form of fats and
sugar. 'Combustion' is made possible by the oxygen taken in by
respiration. There are, however, physiological limits to this
combustion. Numerous observations have been carried out
which show that a fish can sustain the maximum speed of
which it is capable for a short time. The muscular fatigue that
we notice after great physical exertion shows that our 'motor' is
not in an ideal 'machine' to continue carrying out the work
required. Fish feel tired in the same way, but underwater also
some are in better training to combat fatigue than others.
Observing a trout (*Salmo trutta*) and a herring (*Clupea
harengus*) of the same size, we find respective maximum speeds
of 5·8 km an hour for the trout and 2·6 km an hour for the
herring. But the trout rarely swims at this speed and lives rather
a quiet life, while the herring swims tirelessly in search of food.
There thus exists a fairly loose relationship between the
maximum speed, used by the fish only in times of necessity, and
its cruising speed which can be maintained for a period of time.
To flee from the jaws of a predator, quick acceleration is more
necessary than speed. Some fishes have amazing performances:
carp, minnows, pike, cover the first five centimetres, starting
from scratch, with an acceleration of 40 m/sec^2. Over such a
short time, their acceleration equals that of a racing car.

73

The heavy fishes

When a dogfish attacks its prey, the onlooker cannot help noticing the particular tactics it uses. Having singled out its prey, the dogfish begins to move round it in circles until with a sudden dart it is on top of it. This technique is imposed by the structure of the dogfish. The diagram opposite shows that the dogfish's tail is heterocercal (asymmetrical) and that when it moves it generates two forces: one propulsive (1) and the other elevating (2). The propulsive force pushes the animal forwards, while the elevating force tends to lift the dogfish's tail upwards. As a result of this elevating force the snout would tend to turn downwards, but dogfish are able to maintain a completely horizontal position. They counterbalance the impetus of the tail with an upward thrust of the large pectoral fins (3). Their function is very like that of aeroplane wings: the pectoral fins, like wings, produce this thrust only when the dogfish is moving. But dogfishes are slightly heavier than water and if their movement stops, they start to sink to the bottom, like a plane whose engine has stopped. Forced to act as wings, the pectoral fins are hardly mobile. Dogfish find it impossible to stop suddenly and must always be on the move; they can only rest on the bottom where the sea is shallow. Thus their best hunting ground is in the open sea where, on the surface of the water, they find their food and must spend their lives. This force is one reason for their great voracity: they are forced into a life of action and so their need for fuel is continuous.

Weightless fishes

As everyone knows, the goldfish (*Carassius auratus*) spends much of its time motionless in the water if it is not disturbed, and can stay like this without fatigue. How is it able to maintain this stable position in liquid without using its fins? Archimedes' principle must compensate the weight of the fish exactly. But the density of the water varies and the weight of the fish is not constant either. Obviously something must exist that is able to adapt Archimedes' principle to the fish's needs at any given moment. Given that Archimedes' principle depends on the volume of water displaced by the fish, it will achieve perfect hydrostatic equilibrium by modifying its volume, even just a little.

The swim-bladder

The specific gravity of a fish is generally in the region of 1·076. A freshwater fish (the density of freshwater is 1) that displaces 100 ml of water will receive an upward thrust of 100 gr. The volume of the fish multiplied by its specific gravity gives its own weight, which equals 107·6 gr. The result is a downward thrust of 7·6 gr. In order not to sink, the fish will therefore have to increase its volume by 7·6, without changing its weight. This is possible because bony fishes are equipped with a swim-bladder.

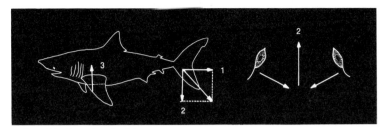

▲ Propulsive forces in a dogfish

▼ Starry smooth-hound shark *Mustelus asterias*

▼ Movement of the pectoral fin of a cyprinid which is staying still in the water

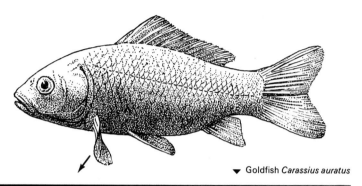

▼ Goldfish *Carassius auratus*

This is usually an elliptical-shaped sac, situated beneath the vertebral column and filled with gas. It is derived from the oesophagus, to which in some types of fish it is linked by a canal called the pneumatic duct. Its size differs in marine and freshwater fishes: in fact sea-water, with its density of 1·026, offers more support. In freshwater fishes the volume of the swim-bladder is around 7 % of the total volume, in marine fishes it is 5 %. The swim-bladder has many forms and can even disappear, as in flat fishes and blennies. If the pneumatic duct is present, the fish is a physostome; if the swim-bladder is separated from the oesophagus, the fish is a physoclist. A

▼ Swimbladders

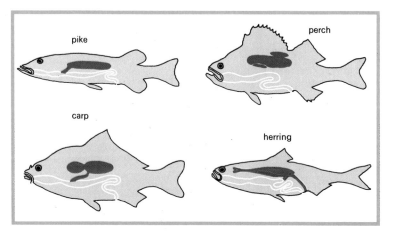

major problem, related to whether the swim-bladder is linked to the oesophagus or not, concerns rapid changes of depth in the water. Changes of depth vary the external pressure, which is felt by the whole fish and by its swim-bladder. There is more danger in coming up than in doing down: coming up, the fish runs the same dangers as a diver, the risk of embolism. If fish who live at a great depth are caught and brought to the surface, they can 'explode'. The physostomes combat this by discharging gas through the pneumatic duct. The physoclists have an epithelium on the swim-bladder which is rich in blood vessels and can absorb or give off gas. Minnows have an external opening of the swim-bladder, near the anus.

Flying fishes

The flying fish (*Exocoetus volitans*) lives in the surface waters of all the oceans in the tropical and subtropical zones. It measures up to 45 cm long, and has large pectoral fins, like wings, supported by strong, flexible rays. When it is frightened, it leaps out of the water and glides along with the help of its pectoral fins. Three phases can be distinguished in the flight of the flying fish: the sprint, take-off, and flight. Before leaving the surface of the water, the flying fish increases its velocity to 25 or 30 km an hour, pushing itself forward with its tail, anal and dorsal fins. When it reaches the right speed for flight, it opens its pectoral fins and bends its body at an angle of 15 degrees to the horizon, so that its head and pectoral fins are out of the water but its caudal fin is still immersed and continuing to supply power. In this take-off phase, the caudal fin is beating rhythmically about 50 beats a second. In order to provide a greater impetus, the caudal fin is modified so that the lower lobe is much longer than the upper one; this helps the fish to keep its tail in constant contact with the surface of the water. Final take-off from the water is assisted by the pelvic fins

▼ Flying fish *Exocoetus volitans*

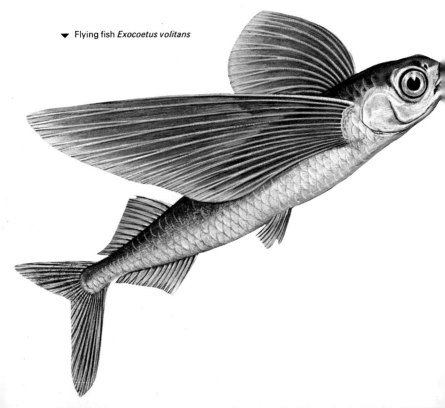

▲ Hatchet fish *Carnegiella marthae*

which, acting as wings, lift the tail out of the water and help it to assume a horizontal position. During flight, the fins of the flying fish are completely motionless. It is not therefore active flight, but a simple, gliding motion. Active flight is practised by the hatchet-fish (*Carnegiella marthae*), and its relatives. They live in South American fresh waters and carry out short flights, beating their pectoral fins like wings. The butterfly-fish (*Pantodon*), which lives in African streams, behaves in a similar way to these fishes.

▼ Freshwater butterfly-fish *Pantodon buccholzi*

Fishes that walk

Many species adapted to a benthonic life have developed pectoral or pelvic fins suited to their habit of remaining motionless on the bottom for much of the time. Many benthonic fishes, however, do not use their fins just to stay still but, like the angler fish (*Lophius*), are able to make little movements by using their pelvic fins. Even more specialised are the appendages of certain gurnards. These fishes have pectoral fins with the lower rays free; these act as tactile and locomotory organs as the fish moves about on the bottom in search of food. The blennies, which have scaleless rather slimy skins, have pectoral fins with the lower rays that are free of membrane at their extremities. With these 'digitate' fins, they can literally walk about on the sea bed. These small fishes live on the rocky bottoms covered with vegetation in all temperate and tropical seas; they are numerous in the Mediterranean where, besides rocky bottoms, they also live on sandy bottoms with artificial rocks such as the breakwaters of ports. The tompot blenny (*Biennius gattorugine*) is one of the largest blennies and measures up to 30 cm.

Other fishes are capable of movement and, unlike the blenny, do not only move about on the sea bed. The mudskipper

▼ Butterfly blenny *Blennius ocellaris*   Tompot blenny *Blennius gattorugine* ▶

▲ Mudskipper *Periophthalmus koelreuteri*

(*Periophthalmus koelreuteri*), for example, lives in the littoral zones of the Indian Ocean, the Pacific and West Africa. Its habitat is the mangrove swamps, trees whose roots go down from the branches and which grows along the coast and can even be half submerged in brackish lagoons. In these surroundings, which are sometimes flooded by the sea, the mudskippers often remain on land and move about by literally walking on their strong pectoral fins, jumping about and overcoming obstacles by thrusting upwards with their tails. Their body is adapted to bear the dehydration caused by being permanently out of water. They protect themselves from excessive dehydration by keeping part of their body immersed in the pools of water left by the high tide. Among the many adaptations to various life styles, there is the extreme case of the garden-eels, eel-shaped fishes, which spend their life in a hole in the sand, from which part of their body emerges just to catch the plankton on which they feed. At the least sign of danger, they immediately withdraw into their holes.

▼ Garden eels

Feeding

Energy and nourishment

To eat and not be eaten is the imperative that governs life in the sea. The life of fishes is one of movement, which leads to a constant demand for energy. Normally these energy needs are satisfied by eating other, usually smaller fishes.

Some fishes eat invertebrates, others miniscule plants or animals, while some species feed on organic detritus or dead animals. This variety of food sources, however, does not mean that the fish has inexhaustible energy reserves at its disposal. There is a point in this 'food chain' at which new matter or new energy has to be introduced. To understand better what is meant by a food chain, it is necessary to take an example: let us imagine an alimentary source that feeds a small fish and that this small

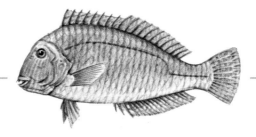

fish may be the food of a bigger one. If the latter is not eaten by anyone, it becomes the apex of the food chain of which it is part. So that the chain may always have new material at its disposal, the base has to be in a position to recycle the materials discarded by the various links in the chain; it must, moreover, be able to obtain of the necessary energy for this process. The ultimate food source that makes up the base of the chain is provided by plants. They are in a position to take advantage of the light energy of the sun, transfer it by biochemical processes that take place inside them, and built new material, fashioned from materials discarded by other organisms. By serving as food for other forms of life, plants re-cycle materials that would other-wise be lost.

The ecosystem

The environment and the relationship of the plants and animals that live in it, to form a vital system that maintains perfect equilibrium in a natural way, is called an ecosystem. We might say that each species has its own ecosystem, in which other species live interdependently. Ecosystems are limited by various kinds of barriers. For example, the spread of a species from one area to another can be impeded by different water temperatures or different degrees of salinity, as well as by obvious physical barriers, as in the case of two rivers flowing into different seas. There are many ecosystems in the sea; in fact, it is so vast that different areas have different kinds of equilibrium. An inland sea such as the Mediterranean or the Black Sea does not have the same kind of flora and fauna as the Pacific Ocean, nor do fresh waters have identical ecosystems. The rule of self-sufficiency is always respected. The equilibriums that regulate this self-sufficiency involve many species of plants and animals and are very delicate. Even the slightest outside intervention can change the physiological processes of the various links in the chain. In fact, to alter an ecosystem you need only alter one of its components; their strict interdependence will force the ecosystem to evolve a different ecosystem, able to cope with the disappearance of the stricken component. This variation can be catastrophic for the initial ecosystem, because the elimination of a single component from an ecosystem that has some hundreds' of species, can upset the equilibrium of all the species present and in a short time lead to their disappearance. Even a foul-smelling marsh is an ecosystem, but the forms of life that populate it are very simple and primitive. To reduce a lake to a marsh it is not necessary to make any radical alterations: a change of temperature caused by pollution is enough to alter its equilibrium. Pollution is more noticeable in fresh waters, especially in those with a small surface. The vast quantity of water in the sea can more easily dilute polluting products, but projects such as the dykes on the Davis Strait between Labrador and Greenland to stop the cold Labrador current and improve the climate of north-east America, could create serious changes in the conditions of the entire Atlantic Ocean. A change of temperature that forced sardines to migrate would also involve all the predatory species that feed on those fishes. Pollution of an area of the sea-bottom would not only affect the animals that live on the bottom, but also all those who feed on them.

To make the interactions that regulate life in the water clearer, the forms of marine life are subdivided into nekton, plankton and benthos. Nekton is made up of those animals able to move actively by swimming; they are fishes, cephalopods (cuttlefish, squids, etc.) and whales. The plankton consists of the myriad tiny animals of almost microscopic dimensions that float passively and let the currents carry them. The floating plant organisms and larger invertebrates, such as medusae, are also part of the plankton. Then there is the benthos, which consists of non-floating invertebrates that live in close contact with the bottom. The benthos is made up of a large group of Polychaeta, marine worms that live in sand or mud, all the sessile organisms (sponges, corals, molluscs), and forms that move mainly by crawling (starfishes, sea cucumbers, crabs, and crayfish). Also of great importance are the bacteria and all the micro-organisms that help to break down the organic detritus; the demolition of organic materials to transform them into elementary or simple compounds that can be used by plants.

Plankton is the most important link in the chain, especially the part made up of phytoplankton. The complex of planktonic organisms is divided into phytoplankton and zooplankton. The phytoplankton is the plant organisms able to carry out photosynthesis, that is, a series of reactions that forms macromolecules from simple compounds using solar energy. In surface waters, which are the sunniest and therefore the most productive, the phytoplankton offers plankton-feeders usable material equal to, if not superior to, the weight of all the plants on earth. This enormous quantity is made up of organisms whose dimensions are measured in tenths of millimetres. The chief components of phytoplankton are diatoms and other minute forms of algae. The density with which these algae populate the sea can at times be so great as to create a serious danger to the survival of the fishes themselves. Some large mortalities amongst fish are in fact caused by dinoflagellates, which become very numerous at certain times of the year. The 'red tides' off the South American coasts is caused by these phenomena: the red-coloured algae are so numerous that they give the sea a burning red colour.

Normally the concentration of algae does not harm the fishes and provides food for plankton-feeders and the zooplankton, which feeds on minute algae.

Many components of the zooplankton are protozoans, or single-celled animals, including the particularly relevant foraminiferans and radiolarians. These are so numerous as to be an important part of the mud on the bottom of the sea. The skeletons of these protozoans sink to the bottom on the death of the individuals and in time accumulate until they reach a considerable thickness. Zooplankton, the second link in the food chain, is the food of many species of fish and of tiny crustaceans and the larvae of invertebrates, which in turn will be the food of other fishes. The large plankton-feeding sharks are direct consumers of plankton, and the fact that they feed on such small animals does not prevent them from sharing the record for size in the whale shark. Plankton is found at all levels of the sea, though it is more abundant in the surface layers. It is moved about by the currents (some vertical movements are the result of variations in the gravity of the animals). Certain planktonic organisms have vertical migration seasons, others move daily, according to their feeding requirements.

The third link in the food chain is the plankton-feeders, some of which are very large. The most important to the food chain are young fish and small plankton-feeders, such as the sardine (*Sardina pilchardus*) and the anchovy (*Engraulis encrasicholus*). These fishes live in shoals that reach and sometimes exceed a thousand million individuals, and they are the favourite food of marine predators from the gar-fish (*Belone belone*), to bulkier predators such as bonitos, tunnies and swordfish. Many predators eat larger fish than sardines and anchovies which, in turn, were probably fed by them.

The marine food chain is very like the freshwater one. The difference is that the latter is much less stable than in salt water

▼ Phytoplankton (above); zooplankton (below)   Zooplankton ▶

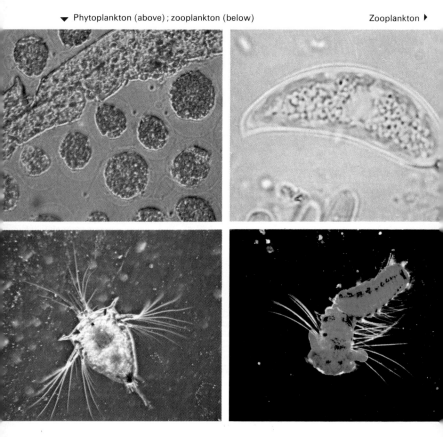

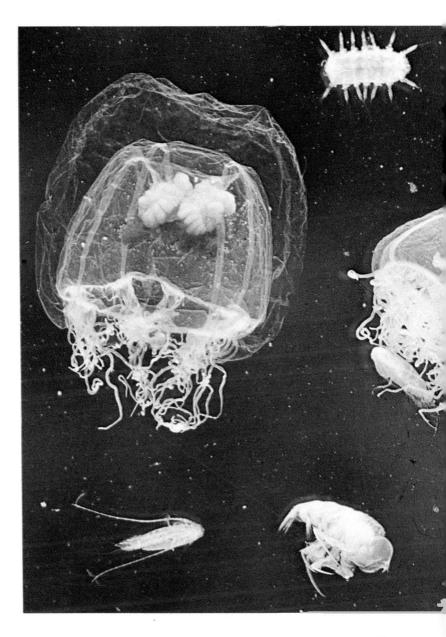

89

and its plankton is therefore different from marine plankton. A fair number of freshwater fishes feed on plants, and many feed on detritus. The carnivores at the top of the food chain are only made up of a few species. Well known are the pike (*Esox lucius*) and the largemouth black bass (*Micropterus salmoides*).

The diagram below shows the interaction between the various species and organisms that inhabit the sea. The food chain is in fact more complicated. The relationship between the species is very complex, and the description here is confined to the more macroscopic effects. The diagram does not include bacteria, which are responsible for the destruction of the organic detritus, an operation consisting of the demolition of

▼ Food chains of the sea

organic substances with a complex composition. This process allows these substances to be diffused in the water, due to their greater solubility, and to be used by plants for the formation of new organic substances. This page shows a very simplified food chain which takes into account the three levels of aquatic life: plankton, benthos, and nekton. The fish at the top of the chain partially returns to the cycle on its death; it will partly be eaten by necrophagous organisms and decomposed by the action of bacteria. Part of the energy lost is replaced by the phytoplankton that sustains the whole vital cycle.

Following this account of the food chain, we must now take into consideration the various components of the chain itself.

▼ Food chain in freshwater

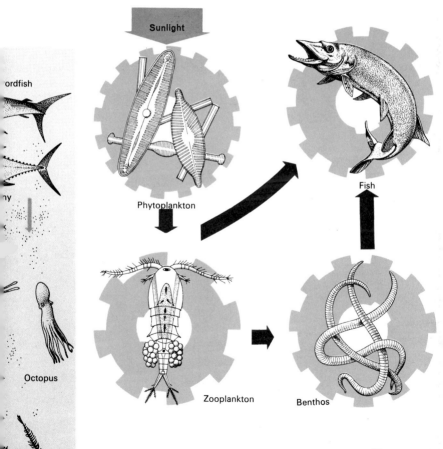

Sunlight

Phytoplankton

Fish

Zooplankton

Benthos

ordfish

Octopus

▲ Anchovy

▲ Sardine

The food pyramid

Part of any plant food eaten by a fish is used by the fish as fuel for its muscular 'motor', and only part is actually transformed by biological synthesis into new 'flesh'. Fishes moreover grow, and in order to take place their growth needs energy and protein, which are produced from the materials taken in when feeding. This is also true of the final predator of the plankton-feeding fish. The predator will eat the plankton-feeder, but will not transform it entirely into flesh. Thus from one link to the next a refining of the food at its disposal takes place, right up to the final link in the chain (the secondary consumers, that is, the predators of predators). Therefore the amount of living things at the bottom of the chain is large; at the top it is small: hence it is called the food pyramid.

Supposing we take a ton of phytoplankton as the base of the pyramid, if a tenth of this amount is used by herbivorous fishes to make new flesh, there will be about 100 kilogrammes of food for each successive link in the food chain. The carnivorous fish will use a tenth of the food taken in to make new flesh, to the benefit of the heavier predator who will eat it, and thus, as the top of the pyramid is approached there is always less available food. In general, a fish near the top of the food pyramid will be bigger than one near the bottom, and the number of individuals of that same species will be considerably fewer than those of a plankton-feeding species.

Man always puts himself right at the top of the food pyramid and often also makes his presence felt in the intermediate phases, thus altering the natural equilibrium.

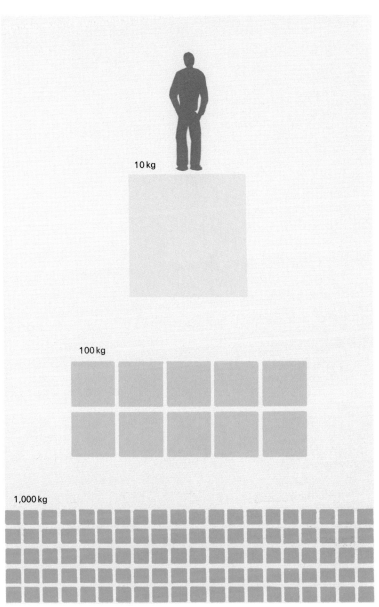

10 kg

100 kg

1,000 kg

▲ Food pyramid

The fight for food

The food chain enables all the inhabitants of the waters to get food. But this has to be caught and, naturally, most of the time the prey-organisms do their best not to be eaten. This gives rise to an incessant struggle for life which each species has developed in the most suitable way. Take the example of a carnivorous predator, the dolphin fish (*Coryphaena hippurus*). A voracious fish-eater, it ruthlessly devours flying fish, which fly out of the water in an attempt to escape from this active predator. But the dolphin waits until the fish drops back to the water. The flying fish often falls into the mouth of the dolphin fish, but it sometimes escapes by rebounding on the water. It is not unusual to see the dolphin fish partially emerge from the water in an attempt to catch its prey.

Many predators, such as tunnies, bonitos, and barracudas, depend above all on their speed when hunting. They usually

▼ Archer fish *Toxotes jaculator*

attack shoals of gregarious fishes and go on eating until they are satiated. Other predators, such as the pike, wait for their prey hidden amongst plants and count more on the element of surprise than on their skill in the chase. The pike, in fact, is capable of making sudden, rapid sprints, but its swimming speed is fairly modest. The adult perch (*Perca fluviatilis*) and largemouth black bass (*Micropterus salmoides*) eat everything they are able to attack. A freshwater fish with strange habits is the archerfish (*Toxotes jaculator*), which lives in the rivers and lagoons of India and S.E. Asia. It swims just beneath the surface of the water and, when it sees an insect settled nearby, it sticks out its snout and by compressing its gill covers and mouth region, spits a jet of water at the unsuspecting prey. The insect, weighed down by the water, falls onto the surface of the water and is immediately swallowed up. The strangest aspect of the archerfish's behaviour is not the unusual way in which it procures its food, but the fact that it is able to take such accurate aim before firing the jet of water at its prey. Considering that the fish takes aim with its eyes under water, this means that it is able to correct any error caused by the different refractive indices of the two media (water and air), a skill worthy of the most highly developed optical instruments. Also in the depths of the sea, where food is not as plentiful as on the surface, several fishes have evolved in an unusual way. The great swallower, *Chiasmodon niger*, which lives at depths of more than a thousand metres, can dilate its mouth and take in prey much larger than itself. Its stomach expands in such a way that it is possible to see the prey through its transparent walls. The sparsity of food in the deep sea has resulted in this fish being able to take in larger than usual food items which will last it for a long time.

▼ Perch *Perca fluviatilis*

The plankton-feeders
It might be thought that plankton-feeders are in a privileged position compared to predatory fishes. But this is not true, because although the plankton is not actively evasive, its concentration varies according to the salinity of the water, its temperature, and the season. In temperate zones, where the changes of season are obvious, the plankton is most concentrated in the hot season, which has maximum sunshine. In winter plankton visibly declines.

The basking shark (*Cetorhinus*), one of the large plankton-feeders of the temperate seas, loses its gill-rakers—a kind of sieve on the gill-arches that enables it to filter the plankton—during winter. The shark is thus unable to feed itself and probably hibernates and as far as possible limiting its movements on the bottom of the sea. At the beginning of the summer season the gill-rakers grow again and the shark can feed on plankton again.

Plankton-feeders usually swim with their mouth open and filter enormous amounts of water, but other fish prefer to wait for their food to come to them like the angler-fish (*Lophius piscatorius*), who moves an appendage which acts as bait to lure its tiny prey towards it.

▼ Angler fish *Lophius piscatorius*   Manta-ray, *Mobula mobular*, a plankton-eater ►

Detritus-feeders and bottom-dwellers

The sea-bed is richly populated with molluscs, crustaceans and other invertebrates. Some fishes have adapted to eat this kind of food by acquiring a typical shape. The flattened body and mouth in a ventral position help the fish to take in food while moving close to the bottom. The wrasses are a good example of adaptation to a benthonic way of life. The guitar fish (*Rhinobatus rhinobatus*), feeds mainly on molluscs, which it crushes with blunt teeth set one behind the other so as to form a continuous surface.

Again in response to benthonic life, certain fishes have developed sensory appendages and protrusible mouths, like the sturgeons, which are equipped with tasting barbels and a protractile mouth that sucks up food like a pump. All the detritus produced by other animals falls on the bottom of aquatic habitats. Thus the bottom is rich in organic substances that are exploited by invertebrates, bacteria, and also directly by certain fishes.

The grey mullet (*Mugil cephalus*), which lives in brackish water but can cope with both salt and fresh water, is a fairly omnivorous detritus-feeder and will eat anything edible it finds on the bottom. There are many freshwater detritus-feeders. The spined loach (*Cobitis taenia*) has sensory barbels around its mouth. A strange fish is *Gyrinocheilus*, from South-East Asia. It is vegetarian and grazes algae from rocks with special rasp-like folds inside its lips.

▼ *Gyrinocheilus*

▼ Spined loach *Cobitis taenia*

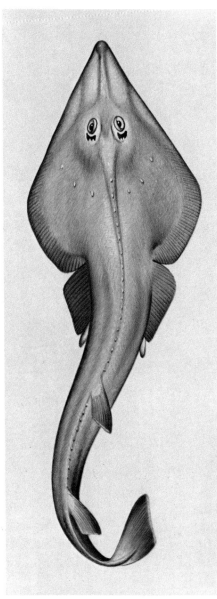

▲ Guitar fish dorsal view

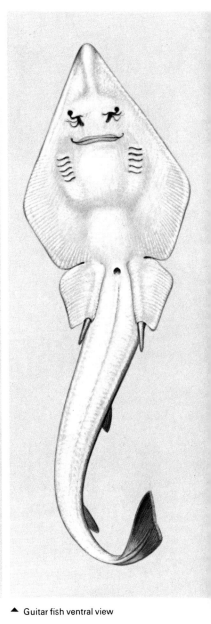

▲ Guitar fish ventral view

▲ *Pygoplites diacanthus*

Coral formations

The coral world deserves special attention because of its variety
of species, its beauty, and above all the richness of the life
there. Coral reefs are made up of the skeletons of innumerable
invertebrates, which over long periods have built whole
mountains under the sea. Rich in crevices and hiding places,
and always sited in warm, clear seas, they have developed a
complex, very rich food chain that attracts many fishes.

   The majority of fishes that live on coral reefs eat
invertebrates. Thus many of them have evolved very strong
teeth and jaws to cope with the hardness of corals, branching
corals, and gorgonians. The polyps that make up coral colonies
are enclosed in a hard shell made of calcium carbonate. These
fish (such as parrot fishes), break off pieces of the colony with

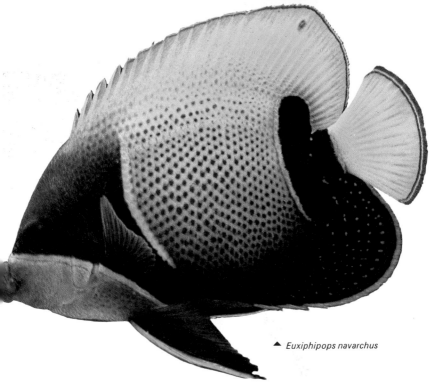

their strong jaws and then grind the food between large, flat teeth, spitting out the calcareous fragments.

The coral world is not only rich in invertebrates; there is also a conspicuous plant life that accompanies and complements the fishes' flesh diet. Thus fishes living on coral reefs have about three times as much vegetable as animal food at their disposal. There are plenty of predatory fishes in surroundings so rich in food sources: barracudas, small tunnies, jacks, groupers, and sharks. However, their prey has evolved defensive measures, they are armed or disguised as protection, and this is the basic reason for the bright colours of coral fishes which pass unnoticed against the many-coloured background. The majority of venomous fishes equipped with defensive weapons such as spines and armour-plating are found in this habitat.

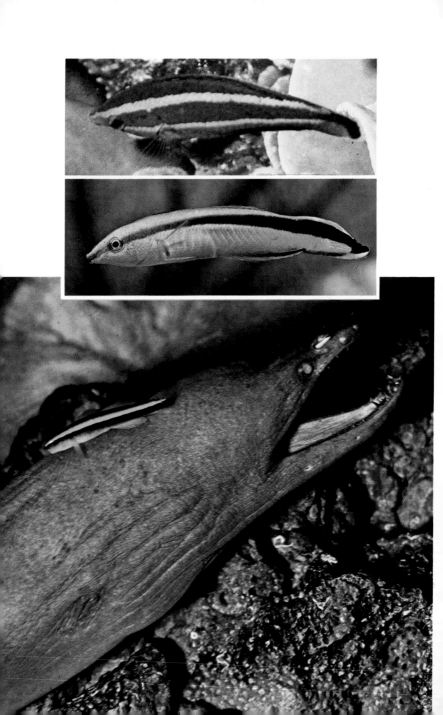

Symbiosis
In an attempt to find sufficient food, some species live in close contact, both taking advantage of the other's presence. This is known as symbiosis. One of the best known examples is the cleaner fish (*Labroides dimidiatus*), which can be seen in the large photograph picking parasites off a large moray eel, the habit from which it takes its name. From the diligence with which the fish explores each fold of its client's body, it seems to be carrying out a very important operation. The remains of many parasites, particularly crustaceans such as copepods and isopods have been found in the stomach of cleaner fishes. These parasites probably come from the client's body, so while the cleaner fish continues in this habit, it is feeding itself and in exchange freeing the other from annoying parasites. Cleaner fishes have many clients and they include species with carnivorous and predatory habits, but the cleaner fish's safety is never threatened. Surgeon-fishes, morays, wrasses and jacks are regular clients who put in an appearance at the place where the cleaner works. In fact this little fish carries out its work in a very precise spot, a kind of 'hairdressers' where the clients line up to wait for their turn. While the cleaner works, the client floats in the water with its fins distended; the cleaning also includes the gills and mouth cavity if the cleaner can enter inside, the cleaner *Labroides dimidiatus*, however, has a rival, which mimics in order to attack the unwary client. This is a blenny, *Aspidonotus teniatus*, which has a very similar colouring to the cleaner fish; the false cleaner is only a little darker than the real one. Approaching the unsuspecting client which, accustomed to the real cleaner fish, does not show any fear, the false cleaner quickly tears off small pieces of fins and skin, which it eats. When this first happens, the fish client may no longer distinguish the real cleaner from the false one and drive away the real one too. With experience, however, the fish distinguish the blenny from the real cleaner and keep it at a proper distance. The false cleaner generally attacks younger, less experienced fish.

Another cleaner fish of the Indian Ocean, the wrasse, *Thalassoma bifasciatum*, has its double, and in this case the mimic is a blenny too. This is *Hemiemblemaria simulus*, which resembles *Thalassoma* in both behaviour and appearance. This blenny feeds on parasites, which it obtains without harming the host, and lives at peace with the wrasse too; the two fish cleaners have been seen carrying out their work together.

Even sharks have their associates: the pilot-fish. This symbiosis is well known, and it was thought that it is the shark that needs the attentions of the pilot-fish (*Naucrates ductor*). The truth is very different: the pilot-fish rides on the wave of compression produced by the shark as it moves and feeds on

◀ Above: False cleaner *Aspidontus taeniatus*
Centre and below: Cleaner fish *Labroides dimidiatus*

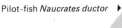
Pilot-fish *Naucrates ductor* ▶

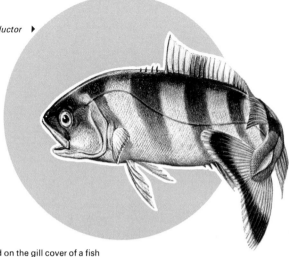

▼ Parasitic isopod on the gill cover of a fish

Remora (sucker-fish) ▶

the surplus of its host. It does not need to free the latter from parasites, so we are not dealing with symbiosis but commensalism. True symbiosis is shown in the relationship between all the great pelagic swimmers and the remoras, or sucking-fishes. They have an adhesive disc derived from the modified first dorsal fin, and stick to the host without damaging it. They feed on parasites; but if they find a place where there is plenty of food, they abandon the host and stay there until they have exhausted the food, when they attach themselves to another host and go in search of a better place.

Symbiotic relationships with invertebrates are also known, some of which are the hosts of certain species of fish. One example is the horse mackerel (*Trachurus trachurus*) and some large jelly fishes. The young fish live under the tentacles of the jelly fish and receive protection from it. These tentacles are

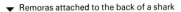

▼ Remoras attached to the back of a shark

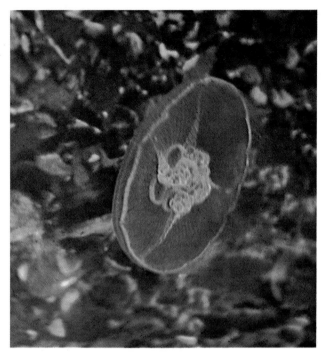

▲ Jellyfish

▲ Scad or horse mackerel *Trachurus trachurus*

equipped with numerous stinging cells that secrete a venom which is fatal to the majority of fishes and painful for man. The horse mackerel is immune to the venom given off by the jelly fish; and in exchange it may help to attract the attention of other fishes. Moreover the horse mackerel feeds on the tentacles and decomposing parts of the medusa and acts as a scavenger. The Portuguese man-of-war (*Physalia*), an invertebrate with a very painful sting, has an associate too, *Nomeus gronovii*. The terms of this symbiosis are rather obscure, for the remains of the symbiotic fish have been found in the digestive cavity of the *Physalia*; but despite this, the man-of-war is usually accompanied by this fish, which stations itself under the floating organ, or pneumatophore, and does not move away.

Commensalism

Unlike symbiosis, in which both parties benefit from the association, commensalism gives advantages to only one of the partners, though without harming the other. Some gobies, for example, live in galleries inhabited by crustaceans. The blind Californian goby (*Typhlogobius californiensis*) lives in association with a decapod crustacean, and feeds on the surplus of the host and on what the currents of water bring into the gallery. The arrow goby (*Clevelandia ios*), a little fish from the American shores of the Pacific Ocean, are guests in the galleries of a worm (echiuroid) and can live with crustaceans, which they help to catch food.

▼ Castor-oil fish or escolar *Ruvettus pretiosus*

Parasitism

A particular form of evolution in the strategy of acquiring nourishment is parasitism. This adaptation results in considerable changes in the characteristics of the parasitic animal and more or less serious damage to the tissues of the host, which in some cases may even cause death. The pearl-fishes are parasitic fishes which have evolved a long, thin shape that allows them to live in the lower parts of the host's intestine. Invertebrates such as sea cucumbers, are the favourite hosts of *Carapus acus*, a pearl-fish which lives in the Mediterranean. Other species are parasites of bivalves and tunicates. Pearl-fishes do not lead totally parasitic lives; when adult, they behave more like lodgers than parasites. It is probable that these parasitic fishes alternate both forms of behaviour according to the feeding possibilities available and the type of host which they live with.

Feeding migrations

In their perennial search for food, fish sometimes carry out regular migrations of considerable importance. The plankton-feeders, for example, are forced to follow all the moves of their planktonic food, as it is carried by currents. The plankton, moreover, makes considerable vertical migrations, varying in magnitude according to the amount of sunshine and the temperature of the water, and the fish have to keep up with them. Tunnies, for example, migrate to rich feeding grounds, but are reunited in clearly-defined zones during the breeding season. This dispersal is related to the search for food, represented by small fishes in turn dependent on the distribution of plankton for their food. This often results in local migrations. In fact, many tunnies normally found near the coasts do not go far when they disappear; they move into water of considerable depth. Some species that live at great depths carry out a daily migration to the surface, which is usually related to feeding. One species of Gempylidae, the escolar (*Ruvettus pretiosus*), lives at a depth of about 800 metres during the day, while at night it rises to the surface to eat and can easily be caught by putting lights on the sides of boats. Those species which live at great depths sometimes carry out large migrations without reaching the surface. They may be prevented by the excessive changes in pressure; in fact some fish which live at great depths only come to the surface when dead or dying and are seriously damaged by the decrease in pressure. The escolar, which makes regular vertical migrations, has a curious adaptation: it is equipped with a swim-bladder but to give it additional buoyancy its body is made up of about 30% fat. Sharks that live at considerable depths have massive oil-filled livers for the same reason.

Fish feeding on a broken sea urchin ▶

Reproduction

The continuation of life

Having resolved the feeding problem, every animal finds itself exposed to other problems of survival. Enemies and natural events are equally selective and life would soon be extinguished if the reproductory function were not sufficiently effective. Fish appeared on Earth when life had already existed for millions of years, and evolved by elaborating the reproductive scheme of invertebrates. The sexes are usually separate in fish, but normally hermaphrodite species are known. Males develop sperm in their testes, and it consists of spermatozoa capable of

swimming and briefly resistant to the external environment. The female genital apparatus consists of an ovary where the eggs mature, but it differs according to the type of reproductive system adopted. Fish can be oviparous, ovoviviparous or viviparous, with many intermediate stages. The oviparous fishes, which are in the majority, deposit their eggs outside, where the male adds his sperm to them. In this way, fertilisation is to some extent a matter of chance and the possibility that some eggs will not be fertilised exists, as either the eggs or the sperm may be dispersed. In some cases, this risk is lessened by the construction of a nest, or by systems that permit internal fertilisation. The oviparous fishes are characterised by the emission of a surprisingly high number of eggs: in the ling, a fish related to the cod, 28 million eggs have been counted in a single individual weighing twenty kilogrammes. Probably less than 0.01% of eggs actually produce a mature individual, but it is enough if only one egg in ten thousand produces an individual able to reproduce itself to ensure the survival of the species. The oviparous fish produces two kinds of eggs: those that float and those that sink in the water. The difference is linked to the environment and is an expedient to ensure that the greatest possible number of eggs are hatched. Another method for the protection of the embryo is the oviviviparity. In this case the fertilised egg stays inside the mother's body, her genital organs having developed an incubatory sac. Viviparous fishes have gone one stage further, adapting the internal sac expedient so that the egg can be nourished as well as being incubated. These last two methods of reproduction permit the best possible survival.

Embryology and genetics

When in the genital organs, whether male or female, the spermatozoa and eggs differ in their respective cells, some interesting changes take place. In its nucleus each cell contains the code that transmits all the genetic information necessary to the formation and life of a new individual. In the cells that give rise to the egg or the spermatozoa, this code is reduced. In a normal cell, there is an equal number of chromosomes, constant in each species, in which the genetic code is located, but this number is halved in the egg and spermatozoa cells. With fertilisation, the spermatozoa unites with the egg cell to produce a single cell, called a zygote, and in this way the original number of chromosomes is reconstituted. This allows a new individual to receive characteristics resulting from the combination of part of the mother's chromosomes with part of those of the father. The chromosomes are therefore the carriers of the hereditary characteristics, or genes. The process that leads to the reduction of their number is called ovogenesis in the female and spermato-genesis in the male. The connection between the ways in which the hereditary characteristics are transmitted is obvious, as is the fact that a species is not immutable which always repeats itself but can change, thus permitting the important phenomenon of evolution.

After fertilisation, when the zygote is formed, the egg begins a series of cellular divisions or mitoses (see diagram on p. 114). From a single cell it passes by cleavage (from A to D) to a stage of more cells. The blastula then becomes hollow (E–F) and reaches the blastomere stage. At this point, the embryo begins to separate itself from the shapeless mass of cells (G). This is a first draft of the materials, but the genetic code is able to determine the correct development of the embryo, which now speedily differentiates itself (H) In I we can already see the shape of the body and the eyes, while the remaining space will be occupied by the yolk sac. At this point the characteristic parts of the fish, such as the gill slits (M), begin to become clear, and vascularisation of the yolk sac is seen. Finally, the fin folds appear (N). The embryo is ready to emerge from the egg to face the outside world, with only the support of the food of the yolk sac.

Oviparous fishes

The majority of freshwater and marine fishes are oviparous, that is they lay eggs, which also contain the nourishment needed for the development of the embryo. Probably this solution was developed in an attempt to give the greatest chance of survival to species whose young would hardly have been able to compete in the struggle for food. The eggs must fulfil certain requirements; the most important is the possibility of being fertilised: the covering must be resistant, in order to protect the embryo, but it must also allow external fertilisation to take place. Moreover the embryo is a live individual and as such needs to breathe; the egg covering must be able to maintain a certain permeability to external gases, so as to allow respiration, though this can be reduced. Unlike terrestrial animals, who can adapt their eggs so as to reduce the loss of liquid, above all water, fishes' eggs do not run any such danger; there is, however, the problem of how to avoid excess absorption of water, if the eggs are deposited in fresh water. In the mating season, many oviparous species migrate until they find the best possible conditions for depositing their eggs. The main requirements are the right temperature and level of salinity, and the absence of enemies. The eggs are fundamentally of two types: floating or submerged. If they are floating, they are found near the surface of the water, exposed to the waves and sunshine and at the mercy of currents; submerged eggs enjoy more stable surroundings, but they are probably not so well supplied with planktonic food, which all young fish need. Normally the majority of marine fishes start their lives in an egg drifting near the surface. Life for young flatfishes (Pleuronectidae and Psettoditae) begins as part of a vast throng. A plaice (*Pleuronectes platessa*) can lay as many as 350,000 eggs. This vast number of eggs, each with a diameter of less than a millimetre, rise to the surface because of their gravity, which is less than that of the sea-water, and are dispersed by the currents and winds.

The flounder (*Platichthys flesus*), also common in Italian seas, lays a million and a half eggs. After about seventeen days, unless in the meantime they have fallen victim to plankton-feeders, the eggs hatch and the larvae emerge, which are about five millimetres long. They are translucent, and they still have their yolk sac, a reserve of food that allows them to live for another eight or nine days without feeding. The eggs float because of the swim-bladder and oil-globule, a cavity filled with a liquid that is

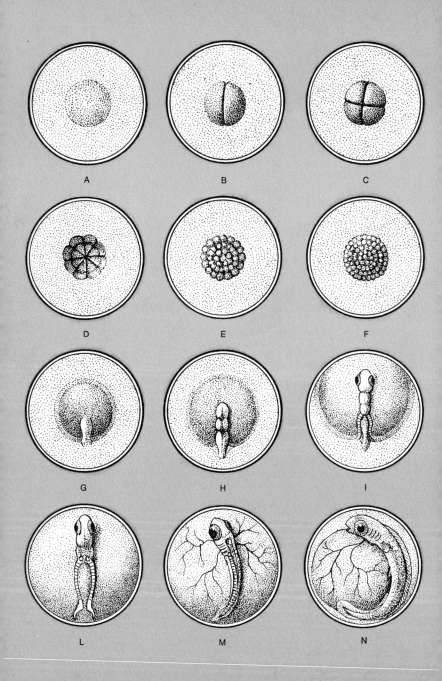

A B C

D E F

G H I

L M N

◀ ▲ Left and above: Development of an oviparous bony fish

lighter than water. Twenty-five days after the eggs have been
layed, the young flounders begin their independent life, feeding
on diatoms. By this stage, the majority of the eggs layed has
already been eaten. Moreover, in all probability, less than 1 %
of the young individuals will reach maturity.

Not all the eggs layed by marine fishes are pelagic and thus
exposed to drastic mortality. Some species attach their eggs to
the bottom or to vegetation. Many cartilaginous fishes have
characteristic eggs equipped with horns, or tendrils, with which
they are anchored to submerged vegetation. Typical of this
type is the large spotted dogfish (*Scyliorhinus stellaris*), whose
eggs seen against the light, reveals a miniscule individual with a
plentiful supply of yolk. The rays (*Raja* sp.) also lay eggs which
are usually attached to the bottom rather than floating.

Normally the number of non-floating eggs produced is much
less than the number of floating eggs. Evidently submerged
eggs run less danger than the floating ones and are
undoubtedly less at risk of dispersion. In fresh water, where the
surroundings are more stable, the eggs deposited are always
submerged and usually attached to the vegetation or in the
sand on the bottom. This method is essential in rivers if the
current happens to be strong. Apart from being dispersed, if
the eggs and larvae were carried by the current, they might be
subject to changes of temperature which could be fatal. After a
couple of months the larvae of the rainbow trout (*Salmo
gairdneri*) hatch but remain in constant contact with the
bottom because they are still only partially capable of
movement and have a large yolk sac. The perch (*Perca
fluviatilis*) lays eggs in strings which are attached to vegetation
or stones.

The eggs of the plaice, which float near the surface, are
exposed to sunshine which elevates the temperatures. They are
transparent, which suggests that the sunlight simply passes
over them without being retained. Trout's eggs, however, are
opaque and would retain the heat given off by the sun's rays;
this may be another reason why trout eggs are buried in the
river bed. In fact, if the eggs or larvae of the trout are exposed
to direct sunlight, it can cause the death of the individual.

115

Generally eggs that develop in fresh water need greater care than those that develop in the sea. This problem has forced many species to develop sexual behaviour including parental care, which can involve the building of nests, the care of offspring and, as seems to be the case with catfish, the instruction of the offspring itself. The seahorses and the pipe-fish (*Syngnathus acus*) present a strange example in the care of offspring. The male seahorse has on its trunk a pouch formed by the protrusion and fusion of the skin. The female lays her eggs in the male's pouch, where they remain until the young are fully developed. This solution allows an oviparous species to behave as though it were viviparous. The newborn young are completely independent from their first contact with their surroundings and do not have to carry a cumbersome yolk sac with them. An even more refined solution is presented by deep-snouted pipe-fish (*Syngnathus typhle*), which live in the eastern Atlantic Ocean. Like other pipe-fish, the male has a pocket made of two folds of skin along the lower part of the tail. In this pocket the fertilised eggs are surrounded by a richly vascularised membrane, a kind of placenta, from which the baby fishes can absorb food and oxygen. After three weeks the mucous membrane is expelled and the young pipe-fishes are quite independent.

Ovoviviparous fishes
The possibility of giving birth to well developed offspring able to move and soon to feed themselves reduces the probability of the larvae ending up victims of adverse surroundings or of predators. The ovoviviparous state has undeniable advantages: the newborn young are like adults in every way, except for their size, and are completely self-sufficient. They do not have a cumbersome yolk sac to hinder their movements and are therefore better at swimming and can resist currents and flee from predators. Many types of cartilaginous fishes including both sharks and rays are ovoviviparous. Probably the survival of a group as old as the cartilaginous fishes is largely because of their reproductive system, which secures a higher percentage of viable offspring than has been proved in the case of unprotected eggs.

In ovoviviparous cartilaginous fishes, the egg is fertilised internally and the male thus requires copulatory organs, which are particularly prominent in rays and chimeras. These 'claspers' are formed by the modification of the middle rays of the anal fins. Some species of bony fishes of the genus *Sebastes* are ovoviviparous because the female has an ovary with incubatory functions, in which the eggs grow until they fully develop. In some rays, the fertilised egg is covered with a horny shell, not as thick and rigid as that of oviparous species, and is retained in the oviduct, where it develops, but without placentary connections. The yolk sac is rather reduced and the

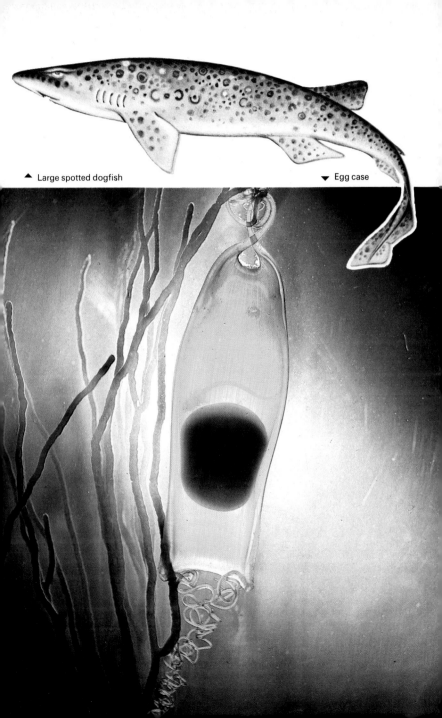

Large spotted dogfish ▲   ▼ Egg case

▲ Gravid male seahorse   Birth (above) and newborn young (below) ▶

embryo secures food through a secretion of the uterine wall. In the embryos of the butterfly ray, *Gymnura*, a long hairy appendage (the hair are cellular evaginations) penetrates the shell, then enters the oral cavity via the spiracle and the pharanx of the embryo, bringing the food and oxygen needed for development. Bony fishes have oviparous and ovoviviparous species, in the same family. The half-beaks are oviparous when marine, but those that live in fresh water are ovoviviparous. The Brotulidae, too, have both forms of reproduction; they are bottom-dwelling marine fishes in which the ovoviviparous species feed the embryo with secretions from the ovary and with special exchange organs that develop in the anal zone.

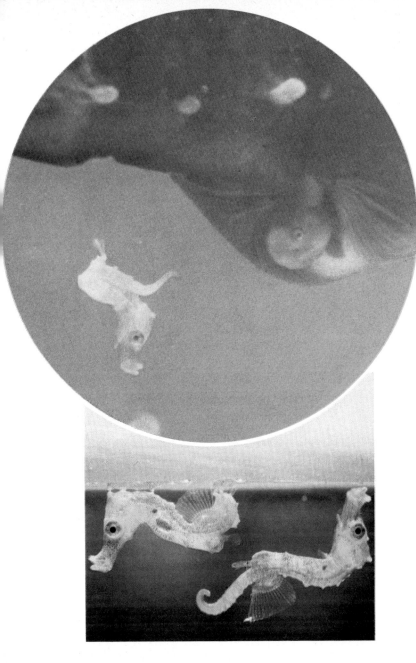

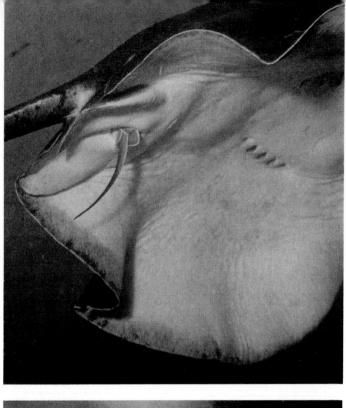

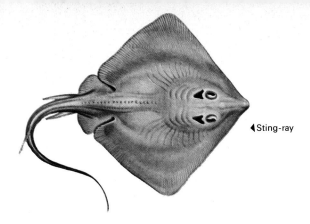

◀ Sting-ray

Viviparous fishes
Some species of cartilaginous fishes, such as the blue shark
(*Prionace glauca*), the hammer-head sharks and smooth-
hound, are viviparous. This is often confused with the
ovoviviparous state, but there are substantial differences.
Viviparous fishes have a special organ that develops level with
the uterus: this is the placenta, which supplies nourishment and
oxygen to the embryo. It is important to distinguish
ovoviviparous from true viviparous fishes, in which the net
weight of the embryo increases from the moment of
fertilisation up to birth. The viviparous species have various
structures adapted to feed the embryo; all, however, have a
pocket communicating with the uterus, which has richly
vascularised walls, rich in folds and excrescences that increase
the exchange surface with the yolk sac placenta, which is linked
to the embryo by an umbilical cord. This structure can be
compared to the yolk sac of oviparous fishes, which has been
modified into a structure absorbing nourishment and oxygen
from the walls of the uterus. In the smooth hound and blue
shark this is attached to the uterine wall. The Spurdog, *Squalus
acanthias*, the best-known small shark of European seas, is
viviparous but does not have a yolk sac placenta. The embryos
feed on infertile eggs, which they find in the oviduct. In forms
without the yolk sac placenta, or where it is not well developed,
the modified walls of the uterus secrete a kind of nutritive
liquid that is absorbed by the embryo through the epithelium
of the yolk sac. The young individuals are born after a long
period of gestation that can last several months. The newborn,
however, are immediately self-sufficient and have no need of
parental care. The number born varies, with an average of four
to six individuals. Because most sharks live in schools
containing only one sex, an adaptive mechanism has developed
that allows females to remain fertile for several pregnancies,
even after being fertilised only once by the male. This has
perhaps evolved to overcome the lack of meetings between
individuals of both sexes.

◀ The birth of a sting-ray

Male guppy *Poecilia reticulata* ▶

▼ Comber *Serranus cabrilla*

Self-fertilisation

When the genital organs consist of both ovaries and testes together it is known as hermaphroditism. This condition, contrary to what it may seem, has come about as an evolutionary stage from the more normal condition of separated sexes. Probably the self-fertilisation mechanism guarantees the possibility of reproduction even in cases where encounters between individuals of the same species and the opposite sex are not very frequent. Actually some species resort to self-fertilisation only in cases of necessity, such as isolation, but it seems that even in their normal surroundings self-fertilisation may take place. Hermaphroditism has been observed in the sea perches, Serranidae and sea breams, Sparidae, very common fishes throughout the Mediterranean and in many other seas. The comber, *Serranus cabrilla*, is one of the commonest hermaphrodites. In the breeding season it

122

can expel eggs and sperm at the same time. The belted sand fish, *Serranus subligarius*, of the American coasts, reproduces by cross-fertilisation: when two individuals couple, the sperm of one fertilises the eggs of the other and each functions as male and female at the same time.

Some experiments with killie fishes have also confirmed beyond doubt the self-fertilisation of these fishes. When some *Rivulus marmoratus* were raised in captivity, they produced eggs, but did not deposit them. Functional ovotestes form in them. An isolated individual deposited fertile eggs which, in turn, were isolated. A young fish born from one of these eggs was brought up in isolation and after some months it too laid eggs which were again isolated and which hatched regularly, producing new individuals. The latter, separated from each other, gave fertile eggs to the successive brood.

▲ *Symphodus tinca*—normal coloration

Breeding colorations

At the time of reproduction fish of many species, particularly freshwater ones, assume colours differentiating their sex. The males particularly tend to be more brightly coloured. Many species, moreover, show a difference in size between the male and female: usually the female is smaller, though there are many exceptions. These differences between the sexes are called sexual dimorphism, and are often accompanied by displays in the breeding season.

▼ *Symphodus tinca*—breeding coloration

Sexual behaviour of sticklebacks

The three-spined stickleback, *Gasterosteus aculeatus*, lives in open areas in fresh water in the northern hemisphere, does not exhibit excessive aggressiveness, and is normally not coloured in particularly brilliant hues. It behaves like other gregarious freshwater fishes. At the time of breeding however, its behaviour changes completely: it leaves the open water (see p. 126, 1) and starts to look for calm waters. Here, he abandons his peaceful behaviour and fights furiously any other stickleback which tries to enter its territory, particularly members of its own species (2). In these battles he reveals a strong sense of ownership and curious behaviour. If he fights another stickleback who has settled near his territory, he is more aggressive the nearer he is to his nest. Let us consider two sticklebacks, one of whom is near his nest and the other further away. The first will undoubtedly be more combative than the second, who will quickly retreat towards his own nest. Approaching the latter, the second gains new strength and routs the other stickleback, who seems less brave away from his nest. This see-saw can be repeated several times. Having defined his territory, the stickleback begins another very apparent transformation: his colour takes on very bright hues, with a red area on the throat and belly while the rest of the body becomes white with blue back. The importance of this livery has been proved in some experiments. If a female stickleback is placed in front of a red object, the same result occurs as with a real stickleback. Like the female, the male is influenced by colour and hurls himself at everything red he sees, seeing in such colour another male, probably a rival. The male stickleback begins to build a nest in his territory by digging a hole on the bottom (3), not too deep. Then by gathering some aquatic plant matter and binding it with a secretion emitted by the temporarily modified kidneys, he begins to build a kind of tube (4–5) wide enough to contain the female with her head and tail sticking out. During this period the male is completely oblivious to the female. Only when he has finished building the nest does he begin to look for a female. Unlike the male, the female does not display any special coloration. The meeting of male and female provokes a pre-determined ritual, made up of characteristic movements and positions aimed at persuading the female to follow the male (6). Finally he guides the female towards the nest (7). When they arrive, he mimes the entry of the female into the nest (8), then retreats and induces her to enter, helping her with thrusts and pinches on the tail (9), which help the female to lay her eggs. When laying has finished, the male drives her out of the nest and enters himself to fertilise the eggs (10). This ritual is repeated many times and with several females, until there are up to five different broods. Sometimes the male builds more nests. When the egg-laying phase has finished, the male takes

Overleaf: The breeding behaviour of the three-spined stickleback ▶

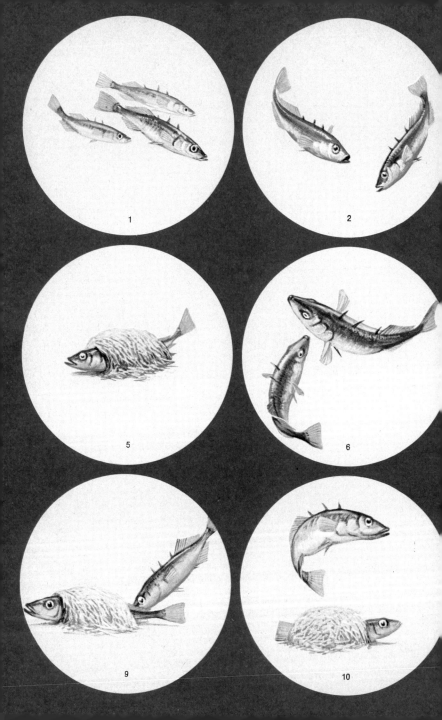

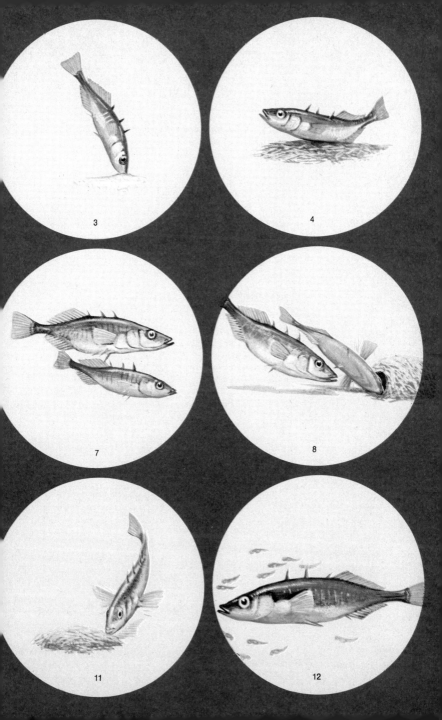

on a darker colouring and loses all desire to mate. But his care of the eggs increases; by moving his fins, he fans a current of air into the nest (11). After the stickleback has spent seven or eight days on guard in front of the nest, the young fish emerge from the eggs and follow their father, who takes care of them and watches over them for about a fortnight, until the young are old enough to have developed the schooling instinct (12).

Fighting fish

In the fresh waters of Africa and South-East Asia live several fish of the family Anabantidae, which have respiratory organs linked to gills, thus allowing them to breathe atmospheric oxygen. One species belonging to this family has a curious feature: the males engage in furious fights that usually end with the death of one of the contenders. This is the Siamese fighting fish *Betta splendens*. In normal conditions, the males are rather insignificant; they have a humble demeanour, with fins folded and dull colours. But when an individual of the same species approaches, they react in a surprising way. The dull little fish gives way to a gaudy red and blue individual with its fins spread and well displayed. This mechanism is a response to the need to safeguard its supremacy in its own territory; if, in fact, the intruder is a female, which is less showy and warlike than the male, the combat does not take place. The female folds up her fins and, if it is not the mating season, goes away. If, however, the intruder is a male, both the contenders, after putting on their 'war-paint', start a series of skirmishes, based on the exhibition of fins and on display. This phase follows stereotyped rules for affirming the supremacy of one individual over another and is typical of many animals. The display consists of a gesture of challenge and superiority intended to humiliate the adversary, a kind of test of strength without actual recourse to deeds, like two fighters flexing their muscles. The display lasts from a few minutes to several hours and, once begun, does not end until the flight of one of the contenders or in combat. Unlike display, the combat only lasts a few minutes; the fishes open their mouth so wide that all their teeth are turned outwards and, using it like a sword, they strike blows at the adversary's body. Although small in size, *Betta splendens* is extremely aggressive and will fight with extraordinary ferocity. At the end of the fight, the losing fish, its fins torn and its body covered with wounds, slowly sinks down, now very near to death.

If the intruder is a female and it is the mating season, the male lets her advance while keeping all his bravura and displaying all his beauty; the female, on the other hand, is timid and submissive. The dance that follows is quite like that of two males, but it does not end in combat. The male has already built a floating nest of bubbles, made of a special mucus. At the end of the courtship, the two fish twine closely

▲ Male Siamese fighting fish *Betta splendens*

together and as the female lays her eggs the male fertilises them. Then he gathers the eggs in his mouth and carries them to the bubble nest, where the young fish remain, safely hidden, until they hatch.

▼ Female Siamese fighting fish *Betta splendens*

▲ Male fighting fish courting a female

Young fighting fish beneath its bubble nest ▶

▼ Female fighting fish shedding her eggs

◆ Sexual changes in Rainbow wrasse *Coris julis*　　　　　▲ Male

▲ Transitional phase　　　　　▼ Female

Sex reversal

Some fishes are not always male or always female. There are some species that, because they are hermaphrodite, never have male and female genital organs functioning at the same time. This is known as sex reversal: the fish leads one period of its life as a male and another as a female. These reversals are usually very showy, and include changes of coloration and sometimes of size. The male or female period can often alternate in the same individual, but in some species the fish born a male then becomes female, or vice versa, without further reversals once it has reached the adult state. Fishes in which sex reversal is accompanied by showy changes of colouring include the rainbow wrasse (*Coris julis*), which is very common in the Mediterranean and, with related species, distributed throughout the temperate and warm seas. These wrasses are less than 20 cm long and live among rocks and fields of *Posidonia*. When they are female, their colour varies from brown to red, with brown or green stripes on the flanks (facing page, top) and they are able to deposit eggs, that will be fertilised by males. If their colour is red or orange instead, with green spots and an orange band, they are males. These are usually some centimetres larger than the females and also older (below). Besides these two sexual types there are also fish of intermediate size and colour, unlike that of male or female. They are intersexual individuals, in which the process of change from male to female is taking place (centre). The colour of the rainbow wrasse is probably influenced by the presence in the blood of special substances and hormones that decide the determination of sex and its change. The change of sex, which one might expect to be limited to a few species, is in reality found in many genera. Another wrasse, the peacock wrasse, *Thalassoma*, has young males and females coloured yellow with a black band along the body. The adult males have a gaudy blue colour on the head. The razor-fish (*Xyrichthys novacula*) also shows the phenomenon of sexual reversal, changing its sex and colour with age, so that the young males and females are pink while the adult males are green.

The Serranidae and Sparidae are two families in which sex reversal is characteristic, in that the young individuals are males, unlike the wrasses. The gilt-head bream (*Sparus auratus*) is male at birth and remains so until it is two years old; then the female genital organs mature and from the age of three on it becomes a female.

Generally the cases of sex reversal derive from an hermaphrodite condition, in which both male and female genital organs are present; the single gonad has two distinct parts and is called an ovotestes. When the female gametes mature first, as in the wrasses, they are called protogynic hermaphrodites. When the male gametes mature first, as in the gilt-head bream, the fish are protandric hermaphrodites.

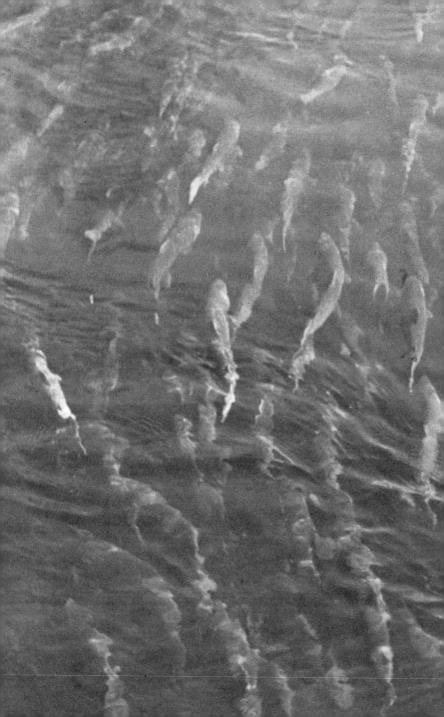

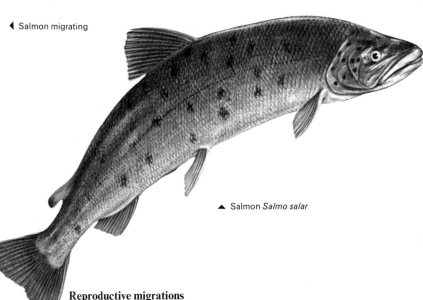

◀ Salmon migrating

▲ Salmon *Salmo salar*

Reproductive migrations

Reproduction is an extremely important event and the search for a suitable place for the young fishes is part of the care taken to ensure the continued survival of the species. Some species undertake very long journeys to find the right place. A special aspect of these migrations concerns animals that during their growing period invade a different environment from that in which they were born. This is the case with eels, salmon, sturgeon and other less-known species, which reproduce at the end of very long migrations in surroundings they have not seen since they were born. Many salmon and eels die immediately after reproduction.

Fish that spend their growing period in fresh water and then go down to the sea to breed are called catadromous; those that go from the sea to breed in fresh water are called anadromous. For example, eels are catadromous; salmon, sturgeon, and shad, anadromous.

Salmon

Probably after one of the glacial periods, the waters of the northern oceans became sufficiently diluted to be invaded by freshwater species. Some species, such as the salmon and its relatives, then moved into salt waters, which were more congenial to their feeding. The Atlantic salmon, *Salmo salar*, is catadromous, that is, 'that it feeds in the sea'. If the adults adapted to marine life, the young did not and probably the reproductive systems did not either; the eggs in fact required the surroundings to which they were by now genetically predisposed. This still applies to the impressive migration of salmon in the breeding season. In the spring or in the autumn the Atlantic salmon ceases to feed. Then it completes the migration that will carry it towards the streams from which it came. Ascending the fresh waters in search of its native river, the salmon often performs prodigious leaps. How it can identify the place where it was hatched has been the subject of many studies, from which it has emerged that it makes special use of its sense of smell, which recognises substances dissolved in the water. The percentage of error in this search for the place of birth varies from 2% to 15%. Having reached the place chosen for breeding, which must have a gravel bottom, the female salmon digs a nest for the eggs. Fertilisation takes place at the same time as the laying, and immediately afterwards the eggs are covered with pebbles to protect them from predators and to prevent them being dispersed by currents. After spawning, the Atlantic salmon returns to the sea and may come back two or three more times to reproduce. The Pacific salmons (which belong to the genus *Oncorhynchus*) die soon after spawning. After a period of time varying from forty to eighty days, the eggs hatch and the larvae come out equipped with a large yolk sac. The young salmon migrate to the sea at the end of three to four years; the young Pacific salmon migrate to the sea after one year.

▼ The migrations of the Atlantic Salmon   A salmon (lower fish) leaping a waterfall ▶

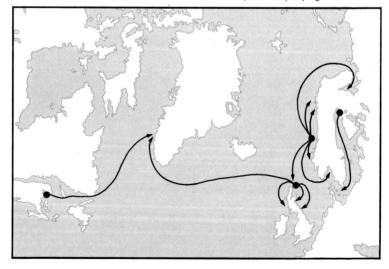

▲ Glass eels

Breeding places and dispersal of eel larvae ▼

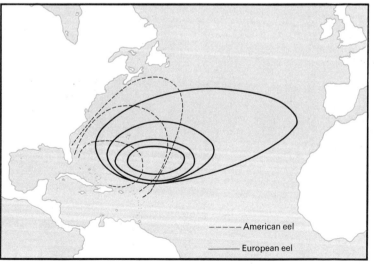

‑‑‑‑‑ American eel

——— European eel

Eels

For many years the breeding migration of the eel was a
mystery, so that popular belief held that they were
spontaneously generated from the mud of pools and streams. It
was only at the beginning of this century that oceanographic
research ascertained that eels breed in the sea and are therefore
catadromous. For a long time, in fact, the larva of the eel was
mistaken for a quite separate species, given the name of
Leptocephalus brevirostris by Kaup in 1856. It proved possible
to reconstruct the migration of the eel by following the route of
the leptocephalus larvae. Fishing for them in the Atlantic, a
Danish oceanographer found that he caught smaller and
smaller specimens as he approached the Sargasso Sea. On
numerous expeditions he happened to catch younger and
younger leptocephalus larvae and others close to
metamorphosis that would give them the definite appearance
of eels. In 1913, the smallest leptocephalus larvae, only ten
millimetres long, was caught. At the same time as this
discovery, Johannes Schmidt ascertained that the larvae caught
in the Mediterranean were always more than 60 mm long and
were smaller near the Strait of Gibraltar. He deduced that all
Mediterranean eels are born in the Sargasso Sea and that the
larvae, partly borne by currents and partly swimming, cross the
Atlantic, enter the Strait of Gibraltar and are dispersed
throughout the Mediterranean. Here, under the name of
Cieche—'blind fish' (an erroneous definition because young
eels can see very well), they ascend the rivers as far as their
most inland waters.

With metamorphosis, the eels take on a cylindrical
appearance (at the larval stage they were flat) and a greenish-
yellow colour, which they retain all the time they are in fresh

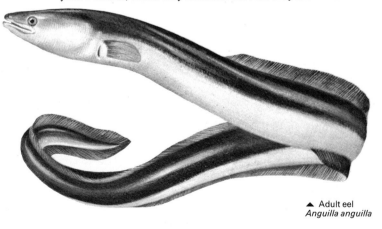

▲ Adult eel
Anguilla anguilla

waters. Legend says that eels are able to travel on dry land in
search of a favourable environment. This is not true, even if
they can move agilely in very shallow water entangled with
vegetation. In the course of the three years it takes to cross the
Atlantic, eels therefore carry out an extraordinary journey.
American freshwater eels also lay their eggs in the area of the
Sargasso Sea, and this has given rise to a theory that they may
be the source of all the different varieties. In fact, European
eels, after a permanent period in fresh water, return to the sea,
lose the yellowish tint that they assumed with metamorphosis,
become silver and their digestive system atrophies. At this
point they ought to return to their breeding area, but in the
Mediterranean the Strait of Gibraltar, the only door to the
ocean, is not crossed by the throng of eels that wait there. For
this among other reasons it was suggested that European eels
never reach the Sargasso Sea and that their larvae are in fact
produced from the eggs of American eels which are carried by
currents to the eastern part of the ocean. This theory has never
received serious support, however.

Many other aspects of the migrations and metamorphoses of
eels still have to be explained. For example, since the average
length of eels at the larval stage is ten times less than that of

▲ Young red grouper
Myceteroperca rubra

adult eels and because larvae more than a metre long have been
caught in deep water, it has been suggested that eels ten metres
long exist. Although this might explain the existence of 'sea
monsters', this has not yet been proved. It is now thought that
these giant larvae are the young of a related group of deep
water fishes, the Notacanthiformes.

Vertical breeding migrations
The conger eel (*Conger conger*) is widely found in the
Mediterranean and has one notable peculiarity. If a female is
kept in shallow water, or for example in an aquarium, at egg-
laying time, she begins to swell immeasurely until she bursts.
Examining the reproductive apparatus, one notes the

▲ Conger eel *Conger conger*

formation of a calcareous plug in the oviduct, that stops the eggs from coming out. This supports the idea that reproduction normally happens in very deep water, where the pressure is great. Conger eels, in fact, have been found at considerable depths of around a thousand metres, and it is also possible to find examples, usually young, close to rocky shores, in crevices and caves just under the surface of the sea. It seems therefore that the eggs or young fish rise to the surface while the adults go down deeper to breed.

Groupers behave in a similar way; their young live just under the surface, usually under drifting wreckage. This behaviour is probably a result of the comparative calmness of

▼ Hake *Merluccius merluccius*

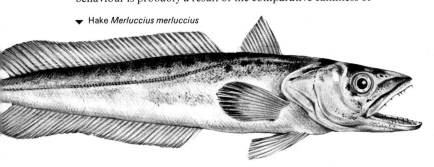

the deep waters, which are suitable for egg-laying, and on the amount of small-size food in the surface waters, which makes them suitable for feeding young fish. Many deep water fishes have eggs or larvae that rise to the surface, from where, having spent their first period of growth, they swim down to the depths, in most cases not reappearing on the surface. The angler fishes (*Lophius*) behave in the same way, as do most species of the cod family (Gadidae) and the hake (Merluccidae).

Differences in shape between young and adults

During growth many fish of various species may display considerable variations in shape. The most striking difference is undoubtedly that displayed by the large group of flatfishes. Plaice, soles and turbots when adult are strongly asymetric in keeping with their bottom dwelling life-style. Their top part is pigmented while the ventral side is colourless, and their eyes are both turned upwards and situated on one side. The young larvae of these Pleuronectiformes are normally symmetric, with their eyes on either side of the head. After about a month of planktonic life, the larvae begin to show an increase in the depth of their body and at the same time a shifting of one eye towards the other side. During this period the metamorphosing larva begins to swim with its body slanted, until it reaches the definitive position when the eye has finished its migration. All this happens in the course of twenty days. At this point the young fishes are heavier than water and begin their descent to the bottom, while their body takes on its final colour. The transformation mechanism is the same in all Pleuronectiformes, with the single difference that some individuals and species are right-sided and other left-sided. In fact the movement of the eye takes place from the left side in dextral individuals, which swim with their right side up, while

▼ A larval sole   Plaice *Pleuronectes platessa* ▶

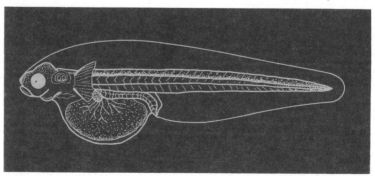

in sinistral individuals, which swim with their left side up, the right eye migrates towards the left side. The turbots (Scophthalmidae) are sinistral, while the plaice and the sole (*Solea solea*) are dextral.

Considerable dimorphism between the young and adult is also displayed by the sunfish (*Mola mola*), which is three millimetres long at birth and has a singular appearance like a medieval mace. Through successive changes the young sunfish's shape alters little by little, until it takes on its typical one at a length of three centimetres. At this point its final growth begins, which takes it to the remarkable weight of a ton and a length of three metres: a real giant!

Many species, while not undergoing metamorphosis, exhibit considerable changes in their passage from the young form to the adult one. Variations are very apparent, especially in pigmentation.

▼ The Cardinal fish, *Apogon nematopterus*, incubates its eggs in its mouth

Special aspects of reproduction

Oviparous fishes practise special techniques for safeguarding their offspring, many of which seem unusual. Above all in fresh water one comes across mouth-brooding, which consists of taking the eggs in the mouth, thus keeping them safe from all possible danger. *Tilapia*, an African freshwater cichlid of the tropical zone, is very abundant a feature which owes much to its care for its eggs and young. Another cichlid, the discus fish (*Symphysodon discus*) of South American fresh water, after incubating its eggs, feeds its young in such a way that it recalls the attention given by mammals. After the eggs have hatched, the young attach themselves to one of their parents and feed on a special secretion present in the skin. For five weeks the young discus fishes remain attached to their parents, even if there is considerable live food in their surroundings. Both parents are able to secrete the 'milk'.

▼ Discus fish
Symphysodon disco

Behaviour

Both marine and freshwater fishes are sufficiently numerous to be sure of coming into contact with other fishes, at least at some time in their lives. These meetings can happen between individuals of the same species or between those of different species and obviously they do not all have the same significance. It is a very different situation for a fish to meet a female in the mating season or a possible rival, compared with finding itself the prey of a hungry predator. Because of the possibility of these various encounters, fish have elaborately planned social lives that follow definite rules.

The most simple situation is meeting a predator; this may be an encounter with one ending only, that the predator eats the fish, but in the majority of cases the prey is able to escape by flight, by defensive weapons such as spines and poisons, by disguises or artificial ways of distracting the predator's attention, or by resorting to the help of another animal. In the sea and fresh waters there are a large number of fish which defend

themselves with spines able to injure the predator: the well-known stickleback has three spines on its back which it erects when attacked. It is easy to see young pike, not yet experienced in the defensive methods of this small fish, struggle with a stickleback in its mouth, suddenly reject it after making a second attempt to it, and then spit it out again at last devoid of life.

Some species equipped with talents for mimicry have developed this capacity in an attempt to avoid detection by a possible enemy, while other species have developed it in order to approach prey unobserved, like the false cleaners (see p. 103). The rays, for example, lie hidden under a layer of sand thrown over their backs, and are almost impossible to detect. All fishes are coloured in keeping with their normal environment: coral fish are multicoloured, pelagic fish are counter shaded (see p. 160). Some poisonous fishes have gaudy colours, perhaps because not being molested by others they have no need to hide, or perhaps to show themselves off, so that they are not taken as food by an incautious fish. Nevertheless relationships between fishes of different species or with organisms of a different kind, such as invertebrates, are not unusual, as we have already seen in discussing feeding relationships (see ill. on p. 167). In these complex relationships, all activities such as the emission of sounds, light, electricity, are significant, and are also forms of communication, though not at the level of the conscious transmission of information. Breeding displays, too, with their ritual, seem to be an intelligent activity of fishes, but if one examines the actions performed on these occasions, one discovers that these are the result of instinctive movements rather than intelligence. The reactions to a meeting with an individual of the same species or of the same sex are very different. There are species that do not display any rivalry, except in obtaining food, about which all fish are in keen competition, and fishes that take part in furious battles or intricate dance rituals with an aggressive meaning. A fight between two individuals of the same species ends with a winner and a loser; the latter, if the fight has not ended in its death, becomes submissive to the winner. Thus a hierarchal order is established, in the same territory, among fishes of one species which, on most occasions, corresponds to variations in their outward appearance. These variations can take the form of different colours, or markings, or the tone of the specimen at the top of the hierarchy may be more pronounced. Moreover, variations in the hierarchy are not possible unless there are new combats or the dominant individual dies. Often the dominant fish will tolerate the presence of a submissive fish, but will attack a newcomer in order to establish its supremacy. What is a fish defending in such combats, whether real or simulated? It seems that many species have a marked capacity for recognising a territory over which they wish to rule. In the stickleback, as we have seen when describing its behaviour in the mating season, the concept of territory is so well rooted that the individual loses its fierceness the further away it goes from its nest. Lacking the incentive of something concrete to defend, its aggressive attitude diminishes, but the fish reacquires it if it approaches its nest again.

Some interesting experiments have been carried out on catfish which show that well-defined social rules exist and that there is a chemical language associated with them. The experiments were conducted with the brown bullhead, *Ictalurus nebulosus,* which when at liberty is a very territorial individual and having marked out an area that includes its lair, firmly defends it against intruders. If two individuals in an aquarium chose the right half and the left half respectively as their territories, they would move about in their territory and, even if they went as far as the border, they would never go beyond it. If one of them was removed from the aquarium, the remaining one would not dare to venture into its neighbour's territory for some time. But if a strange fish was introduced into the vacant territory, the other catfish would immediately venture against it. If the intruder was removed and the original catfish replaced, the separation of the territories would be immediately re-established in a peaceful way. This shows that the catfish is able to recognise individuals of the same species and in particular a single individual. This capacity for discernment is not due to sight, because in experiments where the subjects were blinded, the same reactions were obtained, while there was no response in the case of individuals whose olfactory organs had been obstructed. In tanks where it was possible to confine many fish in close proximity, the dominant individual chose the largest territory, leaving the inferior territories to its subordinates. The majority of fights between these community fishes were confined to a simple show of force and did not reach actual combat. An experiment was carried out to prove that all these responses were due to chemical stimuli received by the olfactory organs: a community of ten individuals was put in one tank, while in another only two individuals were put, which were separated by a perforated barrier so that they were aware of each other but could not come together. If the barrier was removed, the two fishes entered into competition and continued to do so for the next week, during which water from the community tank was pumped in. After the seventh day their aggressive behaviour practically disappeared, and the two individuals behaved like the individuals in the other tank. When the pumping of water from one tank to the other was suspended, within twenty-four hours the rivalry between the two fishes, which were solitary and therefore territorial, reappeared. But the aggression soon disappeared when the pumping of water was resumed for a short period. Also perhaps as a result of a very dry season the fish became very crowded it is easy to find communities of catfishes that live in perfect harmony, and putting some fresh-caught territorial subjects into the same tank confirms the inhibition of aggressive stimuli. This behaviour is very important to safeguard the species, so that individuals who come into contact through lack of space do not attack each other, with catastrophic effects on their survival. In fact, if a normally aggressive individual is put into a community of catfishes, after a certain time it will integrate into the community, which it learns to recognise and acquires a well-defined position. If, however, one introduces a catfish whose olfactory organs are not functioning, there will be a long series of fights, because the newcomer is not in a position to recognise its place in the hierarchy of the community. In such conditions a fish will employ all its energies in combat and will be destined to succumb sooner or later. It has been noted that two territorial fishes compelled to live together sometimes fall on each other so violently that one of the contenders dies; but more often the loser remains alive and, if forced to stay in the victor's tank, becomes very thin, so that it seems impossible that the fishes were originally the same size.

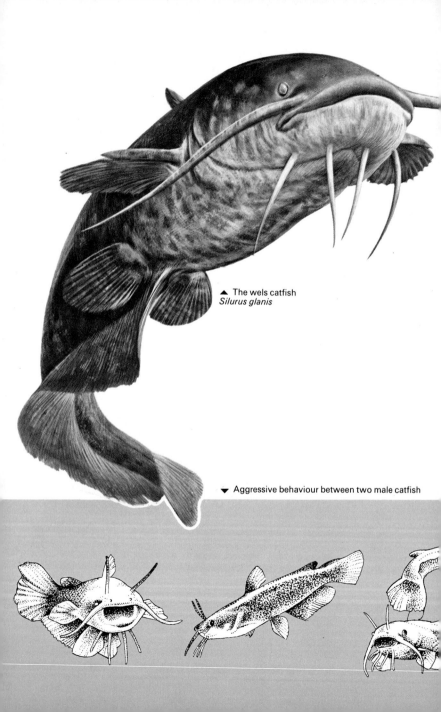

▲ The wels catfish
Silurus glanis

▼ Aggressive behaviour between two male catfish

Encounters between catfishes are not always so violent; cases have been observed in which their behaviour can be defined as mutual. During these experiments it happened that an adult catfish was inadvertently put into a tank containing many small catfish, and it attacked the little ones, wounding them and making them jump out of the tank with fear. Only two survived; left alone, they developed territorial behaviour, keeping to their respective ends of the tank. After about four months, some water taken from a tank that had housed the assailant fish was put into their tank. The reaction was immediate: terrified, the two took refuge in a common hiding-place, concerned only with defending themselves from an enemy that they remembered with terror. Only when the flow of water from the other tank was stopped did they resume normal behaviour and return to their territories. Water introduced from tanks containing fishes that had not previously been aggressors never provoked similar reactions. The experiment showed therefore in the two fishes both the reawakening of the community instinct and the capacity to recognise the smell of the fish by which they had been assaulted. The behaviour of the dominant fish of a small community into which a strange fish was introduced was curious. It was the only one to display aggressiveness in encounters with the intruder and to give battle while its subordinates calmly looked on.

The language of fishes

However inconspicuously, fishes transmit information which is carried by soluble chemical substances in their surroundings, and received by the olfactory organs. These substances are also found in invertebrates, above all in insects. Probably they are only part of the code of transmission, and are liberated by the mucus that covers the animal's body. The urine too can supply information about the fish's emotional state. A subject placed

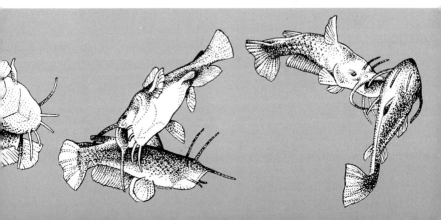

▲ Banded cichlid *Cichlasoma severum*

under stress would have in its urine components which can be detected and interpreted by its fellows. An important discovery has been made in the field of information devoted to chemical substances. This refers to a substance that is released in case of danger, as in the case of an individual member of a community which is injured, this is called the alarm-substance. If an injured minnow is introduced into a tank containing gregarious fishes such as minnows, they will soon show an alarm reaction, and those belonging to the same species as the injured animal will become very agitated and remain so for some hours. It seems therefore that the injured animal releases a substance capable of inducing such reactions. But if a dead minnow is introduced, there is no such alarm behaviour. Similarly, no reaction is seen if an injured fish is put into a tank containing fishes whose olfactory receptors have been destroyed.

The reaction to the alarm-substance is genetically

▲ Oscar's cichlid *Astronotus ocellatus*

determined, it does not have to be learned: in fact it is probably highly developed in the first stages of life. It is also probable that in the first months of life this sensitivity prevents the phenomenon of cannibalism. Not all fishes, however, have such alarm-substances: it is found in freshwater species and above all in cyprinids and characins. The fishes that make the most use of the alarm-substance belong to the Ostariophysi, that is fishes equipped with the Weberian apparatus which includes both the above groups.

Schools of fish
If there are fishes with distinct territorial habits which lead a solitary life and attack their fellows, there are also fishes whose gregarious instinct is developed right from the start. Schools, which are the expression of this gregarious instinct, involve in some species a considerable number of individuals. It is easy to

mistake an occasional accumulation of fishes, caused by abundant food or by environmental factors, for a school. Such a group of fishes intent on feeding crowd together, one on top of the other, will disperse at the slightest sign of danger, which a real school will never do. If threatened by a predator, the school of fishes defends itself by assuming a spherical shape, so as to offer the smallest ratio between its exposed surface and the number of individuals. The dense school may assume an appearance that is capable of intimidating smaller, less aggressive predators.

Living in a school, moreover, means that an individual fish significantly reduces the possibilities of coming across a predator. Imagine a zone of the sea with thousands of tiny fishes and a predator: if the little fishes are scattered throughout the territory, the possibilities that the predator will catch one of them are determined by the size of the territory, by visibility, and by the predator's ability. If, however, the tiny fishes are united in a school, the possibilities of meeting a predator are a thousand times less. Given that a predator, whether it meets the school or catches its prey one at a time, always needs approximately the same daily amount of food, it is easy to see how the school represents a valid defence for its components rather than a well-furnished table for predators.

A school of mackerel, which feed on plankton, when they are in an area rich in food, carry out concentric tours with sudden stops and changes of direction that are so synchronised that they suggest there must be a recognised director hidden in the middle of the school, who directs the manoeuvres. The most impressive thing about schools of fish is the almost perfect alignment of the individuals. The photograph on the facing page, which shows a school of *Haemulon* or grunts, is proof of this regularity of all the components and the school shown is made up of a very limited number of individuals. Usually, schools of herrings or other clupeids contain the greatest number of individuals. A school of fish is not a casual union, but a collection of individuals that observes very strict rules in which the instinct and sensory perceptions of the fish play an important part. Experiments on the behaviour of young fishes have confirmed that the schooling instinct is innate and is perfected in the first stages of life. A fish that becomes isolated from a school when young has difficulty in reinserting itself, and has to reacquire its gregarious character. These difficulties probably arise from the lack of training of its sensory capacities.

Particularly important to fish that live in schools is the function of the lateral line, which is used for maintaining rhythm and perceiving changes of speed and direction. It is easy to see how the simultaneous changes of direction may be

School of grunts *Haemulon* sp. ▶

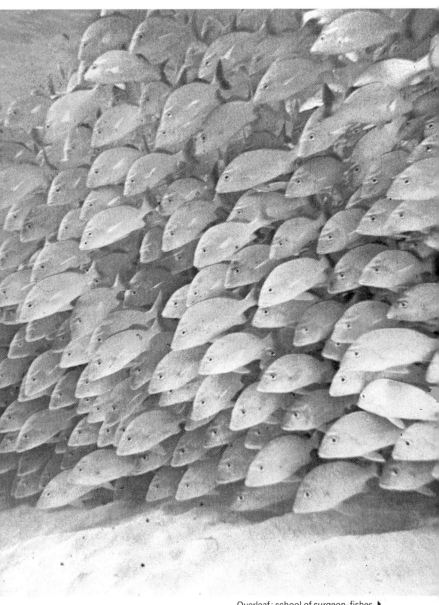

Overleaf: school of surgeon-fishes ▶

assisted by a series of signals transmitted by the fishes, and that the movement of the group indicates the orientation of the majority of its members. Some schools that dissolve at night and re-form by day are made up of individuals that also use their sight to keep in contact with each other.

The importance of colour

If you watch a fish, it is easy to distinguish its back from its belly below not only by its shape or the position of the fins, but also by its colour. The majority of fishes have predominantly light colours on the ventral parts. This is usually more obvious in pelagic fishes which, living in rather uniform surroundings, have a concealing system that uses the effects of the light that falls on their bodies from above. If their colour were uniform, the effect of the light would be like that shown on page 161, above: the back would be light and the belly, in shadow, dark. In which case the fish would be visible even from a long way off. Obviously, therefore, this is why fishes have lighter hues on their belly (see p. 161, centre), so that they are a uniform colour (below) when illuminated from above. This kind of coloration is called counter shading. In surroundings such as coral reefs, where rich colours predominate, few fishes are counter shaded

▼ School of tropical fishes   Coloration of fishes ▶

because of the futility of imitation against such a varied background. Gaudy colours are dominant in poisonous fishes or those armed with spines. In the case of the butterfly-fish (lower photo) the bands or the eye spot on the tail can help to mislead the predator as to the direction in which the fish is swimming. The trunk-fish and the frog-fish *Antennarius* run no danger: the former has poisonous flesh and the latter has tufts on its body which makes it look just like a stone, so that it passes unnoticed. The trunk-fishes, moreover, are protected by a thick bony plating that gives them a characteristic stiffness.

Chelmon rostratus ▼

▲ *Chaetodon plebejus*

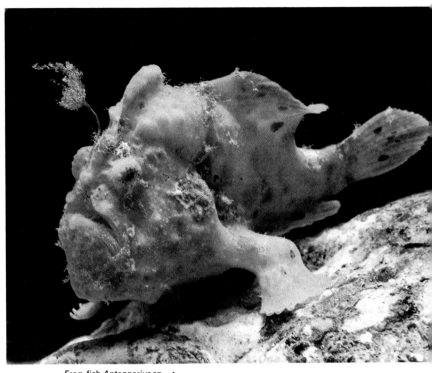

Frog-fish *Antennarius* sp. ▲

Trunk-fish *Ostracion* sp. ▼

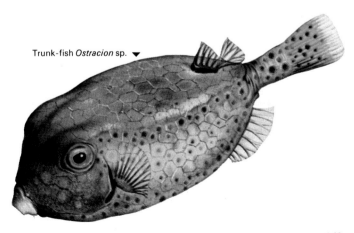

163

Mimicry

Some species of fishes have a considerable capacity for
adapting their colour to the bottom. The colour can vary in a
very simple way. It is contained in the chromatophores, which
are cells under the skin, and it can change in intensity
according to the stimuli the animal receives. Such intensity is
modified by expanding the pigment in all the chromatophores
or restricting it to a small area. If the pigment is expanded, the
colour becomes visible. Fishes which are capable of varying
their colour to a considerable range of tints, such as the
flatfishes (Pleuronectidae), have numerous chromatophores
with different pigments and can imitate with great fidelity the
various colours of even an artificial bottom. Many colours are
obtained simply by varying the inclination of the crystals of
guanine in special colour cells called iridocytes. These act as
prisms, breaking the light up into the colours of the rainbow.
Even fishes who are not particularly imitative can vary their

▼ Scorpion fish *Scorpaena porcus*

colours under the influence of bright sunlight. If some
Gambusia affinis are kept in tanks with bright or dark bottoms,
one will have a progressive adaptation that will be almost
perfect in the space of a few months. An experiment to control
the advantages of such colour adaptation was carried out with
gambusias that had been kept in light and dark coloured tanks.
They were put in tanks of an opposite colour to that assumed,
together with an equal number of gambusias of the same
colour as the tank. Then two predators were put into the two
tanks, and they soon began to feed on the gambusias. The
surviving gambusias which were the same colour as the bottom
of the tank soon outnumbered the others remaining in a ratio
of 3 to 1. The advantages of their colouring were thus obvious,
and they were confirmed in successive experiments. The
mechanism controlling change of colour seems to be controlled
by the sight; in particular, one part of the eye measures the
light falling from above, while another part assesses the colour

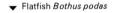
▼ Flatfish *Bothus podas*

of the bottom. The information is transmitted to the chromatophores by special chemical messengers, substances like hormones, and with the help of the hypophysis. The imitative system used by the scorpion fishes is different; they combine a more or less marked colour matching with a similarity of shape to the algae-incrusted rocks of the bottom amongst which they usually live. Many pipe-fishes or trumpet-fishes (*Aulostomus maculatus*), with their elongate appearance, pass unnoticed when they are living among the eel-grass or gorgonians. This kind of imitation of the background is particularly well developed in a seahorse, the *Phylopteryx eques*. This is startlingly like the sargassum weed, the floating algae that lives in large quantities in tropical seas. Thus what seems to be a tangle of algal filaments in natural surroundings is in fact an animal.

▼ *Pterois volitans*

Symbiosis

One way of surviving in a hostile environment is to seek protection near another, bigger animal or one endowed with an outstanding means of defence. Usually the protection is reciprocated by services of various kinds, as in the case we have already seen of the cleaner fish, *Labroides dimidiatus*. One of the best known symbioses between fishes and invertebrates is that of the *Amphiprion*, or clown-fishes, with large tropical sea anemones, to whose usually fatal stings they are immune.

▼ Clown-fish *Amphiprion* sp.

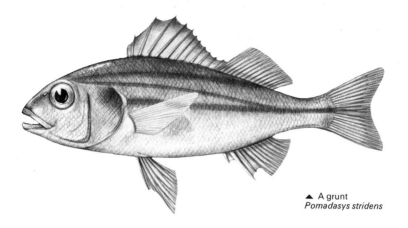

▲ A grunt
Pomadasys stridens

Fishes and sound

From an acoustic point of view, water has outstanding characteristics such as a better diffusion of sounds and noises than in the air. Underwater swimmers can hear the sound of far-off motor boats as though they were much nearer. Fishes are able to utilise this property of water in order to catch the vibrations emitted by other fishes and to distinguish predators from similar, harmless fish. A jack, listening to the noise made by a shoal of small fishes feeding normally, will become very agitated and swim towards the source of the noise. A school at rest makes very little noise, but if it is suddenly disturbed, it begins to make continuous loud noise as it begins moving. Having reached cruising speed, the noise becomes rhythmical, which suggests that it must be caused by the mechanical effects of swimming. Some fishes actually make sounds, like the grunt (*Pomadasys stridens*; above) or the seahorse, for which it seems

◀ Seahorse *Hippocampus* sp.　　　　　　　　　▼ A jack *Caranx* sp.

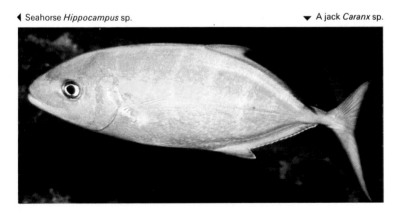

169

the sound may be a sexual signal. The way in which grunts make noises is interesting, as they use special muscles round the swim-bladder to make it vibrate like a drum.

Many species make other noises while eating and show variation of sound producing activity according to the time of day. The North American drum, *Bairdiella chrysura*, and the oyster toad-fish, *Opsanus tau*, and some species of *Pangasius*, South American catfishes, behave like certain birds which make more noise at sunrise and sunset.

Luminous fishes
The sea is not completely dark beyond the zone into which the sunlight penetrates, for there is a weak, pulsating luminosity produced by the animals which live at those depths. This luminosity is at its peak between one thousand and four thousand metres, and is found in all the seas of the world. The fishes that live in this zone have luminous organs, or photophores, which are able to emit light intermittently. The light is produced by different means: either in glandular cells or in special receptacles containing symbiont bacteria. The Stomiatoidei and Myctophidae, or lantern-fishes, produce light from glandular cells. The viper fish, *Chauliodus sloanei* (large picture) belongs to the first, and the *Maurolicus muelleri*, a fish,

▼ Viper fish *Chaulodius sloanei*

which sometimes appears on the surface of the Mediterranean and the Atlantic in certain conditions, belongs to the second. The position of the photophores in these fishes can differ in the males and females. Fishes whose luminosity is derived from symbiont luminous bacteria belong to the rat-tails (Macruridae) and to certain species of deep water cod (Moridae). The relationship between the fish and the bacteria is a real symbiosis: the former gives the bacteria the food and oxygen they need, while the latter provide the fish with light. The reasons for the photophores are several. Possibly in certain species, such as the Macruridae it is used in breeding display. Perhaps luminosity also aids recognition between individuals of the same species and sexes, or helps the deep-sea angler fishes in their search for food.

▲ Photophores

▼ Pearl-sides
Maurolicus muelleri

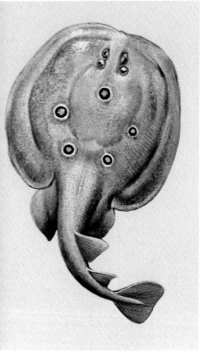

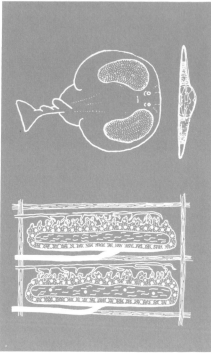

▲ Torpedo or electric ray
Torpedo torpedo

▲ Electric organs of
the torpedo

Electric fishes

Although more than a hundred species of fishes can produce
electricity, only a few are capable of powerful enough shocks to
harm man or other animals. The majority of electric fishes are
found in the sea.

The electric ray or torpedo (*Torpedo torpedo*), a
cartilaginous fish of the order Rajiformes, has two kidney-
shaped organs on either side of the body (see diagram above)
which can emit electric shocks both voluntarily and if
stimulated from outside. The torpedos are common bottom-
living fishes in warm and temperate waters, even at
considerable depth, and the electric shocks have both defensive
and offensive roles, so that prey can be stunned and then eaten
more easily. The electric organs of the torpedo are derived
from gill muscles and are composed of electroplates placed one
above the other to form piles, with a layout very like that of the
elements of a Volta battery. In larger *Torpedo nobiliana*, a
species that reaches 1·8 metres long, there can be a considerable

172

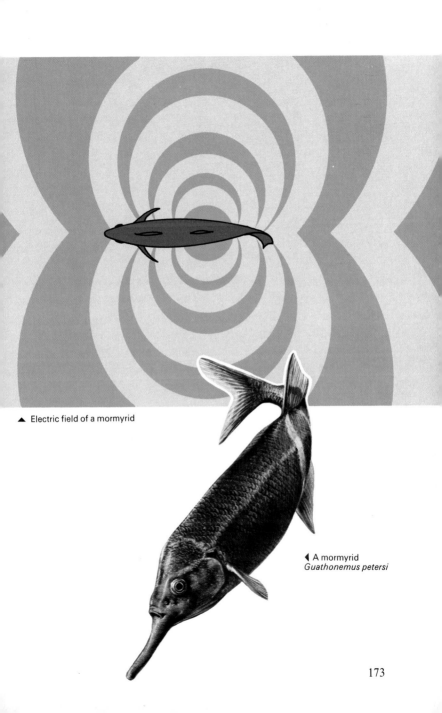

▲ Electric field of a mormyrid

◀ A mormyrid
Guathonemus petersi

173

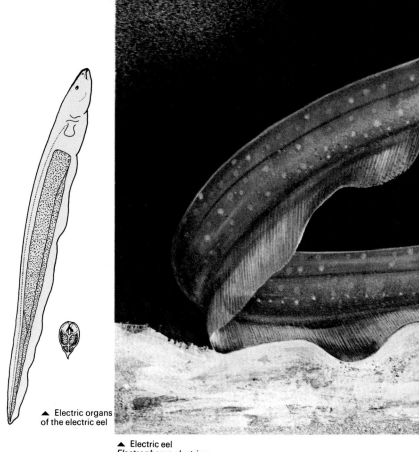

▲ Electric organs
of the electric eel

▲ Electric eel
Electrophorus electricus

number (even over a thousand) of these piles, which are formed
by hundreds of electroplates. If all the plates acted together
they could discharge a very high voltage, but many of the
plates are linked in parallel, thus losing voltage but gaining
strength. The highest output measured in a torpedo was
around 220 volts, but unless the animal is stimulated the shock
is usually much smaller. The electric organs may also be able to
function as a kind of radar in conditions of poor visibility or at
great depths, where light is scarce. Many ordinary rays can
emit similar, low intensity, discharges through muscular organs
near the tail.

One of the more interesting electric fishes is the River Nile
Gymnarchus niloticus, a relative of the African mormyrid which
produces a circular electric field with its centre near the tail (see

▲ Knife-fish
Gymnotus carapo

ill. on p. 173). The field is not constant, with a frequency varying between 6 and 120 impulses a second. When watching the behaviour of *Gymnarchus*, you have the feeling that it can make out obstacles and prey at a considerable distance, even in turbid water.

There are many freshwater electric fishes, some endowed with considerable power such as the electric eel (*Electrophorus electricus*), which lives in the fresh waters of the South American continent. Its discharges reach 650 volts and can stun a horse. It has three electric organs; two are used for defensive discharges and the third, which is weaker, has similar functions to the electric organs of the mormyrids. The South American *Gymnotus carapo*, or knifefish, is very similar to the electric eel.

▲ Cichlid *Tilapia* sp.

The care of offspring

Many oviparous fishes take great care to find the best place to
lay their eggs, but are not interested in the fate of their young.
Normally such behaviour is typical of species which lay a very
large number of eggs with a low survival rate for the offspring,
even in adverse conditions. But there are some cases in which
the parents are concerned about the protection of their young.
We have seen that the male stickleback aerates the nest by
moving the water with its fins. When the eggs hatch, it is the
male again which follows the young until they have developed
a schooling instinct. Many cichlids incubate their eggs in their
mouth and also gather the young there in case of danger (for
example, *Hemichromis bimaculatus*, and *Tilapia*), until they
have reached a certain age. The risks of this kind of protection
are the possibility of being eaten by continuing to take
advantage of paternal hospitality for too long.

◀ Cichlid, *Hemichromis bimaculatus*, with its young

Environments for Living

The underwater environment

This environment, which is naturally characterised by the dominance of water has a greater stability than the atmosphere or the Earth. Numerous animals live in the latter surroundings but they all need to be in constant contact with water. The underwater environment is divided into two types: one salt water, the other fresh water. Between the two is a wide range of intermediate situations that include lagoons, the estuaries of rivers, and inland seas. From the primordial ocean which had a certain uniformity, arose the situation today, in which most species are segregated in well-defined surroundings by environmental barriers, such as salinity or temperature, to which fish are very sensitive. Fishes are called stenohaline or euryhaline according to their greater or lesser sensitivity to variation

in the salt content of the water. Euryhaline fishes can tolerate brackish surroundings and even go a good way up the courses of rivers. Generally they go from a salt environment to a fresh-water one only for richer feeding and they mostly reproduce in the sea. The salinity influences the metabolism and internal water regulation of the individual and is a factor that limits the diffusion of species. The salinity of the sea varies both horizontally and vertically. Maps of the surface salinity have been compiled from isohalines, lines that join points characterised by the same degree of salt concentration. The general direction of salinity is bi-polar; from the point of the equator there is a salinity of around 35 parts per thousand that increases as it approaches the higher latitudes of both north and south. The maximum concentration is in the Atlantic Ocean, around 20 degrees north or south, which has a salinity of about 37 parts per thousand. In higher latitudes as one approaches the polar seas, there is a lessening of salinity with values even lower than 30 parts per thousand. In the seas nearest dry land or surrounded by emerged land, such as the Mediterranean, the salinity is strongly modified by evaporation or by the fresh water from rivers. In seas surrounded by cold or rainy lands the salinity drops sharply because of the fresh water diluting the sea. Thus some parts of the Black Sea and the Baltic Sea have a salinity of less than 3 parts per thousand In the seas where evaporation is predominant, as in warm seas, there is an increase in salinity. In the Mediterranean the salinity increases from a minimum of 37 parts per thousand in the area of Gibraltar little by little eastwards until it reaches 40 parts per thousand near the coast of Syria. A concentration of 46 parts per thousand is reached in the Red Sea, a record for all Earth's open seas. Among the inland seas, the Dead Sea has the maximum density, with an average concentration of 240 parts per thousand. Its waters are so dense that a man can float without any effort and no fishes live there.

The vertical variations of salinity are caused mainly by the fact that the majority of saline waters are heavier and lie under the lighter, less salt ones. This phenomenon is more evident near coasts, where the cold or fresh waters may be stratified above the salt water; in the case of colder, less salt water the stratification of warmer salt water on top is possible.

Temperature is the second variable that influences the underwater environment in both the sea and fresh water. The temperature on the surface rises because of exposure to the sun and the higher temperature of the air, but it decreases from the tropics to the polar seas. The lines on maps joining points of the same temperature are called isotherms, and their course is almost parallel to the geographical parallels. The waters are subject to a seasonal temperature change that is definitely higher in the less extensive, shallower ocean basins, and in fresh waters. The water reacts in a special way to density, which is greater at a temperature nearest to 4°C. This phenomenon causes complex stratification in the course of seasonal variations and currents, and of the water density in different parts of the globe. The cold waters of the polar cap descend at depth towards the equator, while the warm waters move on the surface from the equator towards the poles.

The temperature usually changes little by little from the sea bed to the surface; but this does not always occur uniformly. In the summer, atmospheric conditions produce a thermal barrier (thermocline); the top layers heat up, while those underneath stay at the same temperature. In the winter months, however, a uniform temperature is usually established in the latitudes corresponding to the temperate zones; this is because of the insufficient heating of the top layers, which remain at the temperature of the deeper layers. In the Mediterranean, the temperature at depth is around 13°C and stays there nearly all the time. This is because of the lack of depth compared to the bottom of the Atlantic, and the Strait of Gibraltar, which being shallow allows only water with a temperature of 13°C or higher to enter from the Ocean. In the winter months, the surface temperature of the Mediterranean is the same as that of the bottom, which goes down to 4,600 metres. The life of fishes is linked to temperature in various ways: besides having a direct effect on their metabolism, it also influences the movement of food such as plankton, and determines how much is produced. Fishes who are able to bear changes of temperature are called eurythermic; those who are linked to definite narrow temperature conditions are stenothermic. Like salinity, temperature has a considerable influence on the distribution of the marine fauna and flora. Certain habitats, such as coral reefs, are only found at certain latitudes, and many fishes such as tunnies migrate in search of certain essential temperature conditions. The alternation of the seasons in the inland seas, which are more sensitive to variations in temperature, mean that they are inhabited by a fauna which is adapted to a period of inactivity or limited growth in the cold season, with quick growth and reproduction in hotter periods.

The currents
The phenomenon of currents is closely linked to the variations of temperature and salinity. It consists of the movement of immense quantities of water over quite considerable distances. The most obvious effect of the currents is due to the different temperatures between the transported water and the surrounding water. Warm water in cold zones considerably modifies the local flora and fauna and affects not only the marine environment. The phenomenon is so vast that it involves the climate of the coastal zones. The Gulf Stream, for example, modifies the climate of many European countries and influences a very wide area of the north Atlantic Ocean. Off the United States coast it has a capacity of more than 55 million cubic metres a second. The cold current of Peru impressively modifies the environmental conditions of the Pacific Ocean along the coast of North America. The presence of this current, which is also determined by the wind changing from the land towards the sea, produces upward movements that make this cold water rich in mineral salts come to the surface from the sea bed. In these waters the plankton that feeds immense shoals of fishes is abundant, above all, the anchovies that have produced a vast fishery and fish products industry and are also the favourite food of marine birds. In certain years the decreased force of the winds lessens the cold current, and produces less food for the plankton and, in consequence, for the anchovies.

The currents play a directing role in the transport of larvae and eggs and also influence fishes able to swim actively.

Circulation and productivity of the oceans

    Poorly conductive central waters
    Antarctic convergence
    Zone where Antarctic and Arctic waters meet
    Deep water coming to the surface near the equator

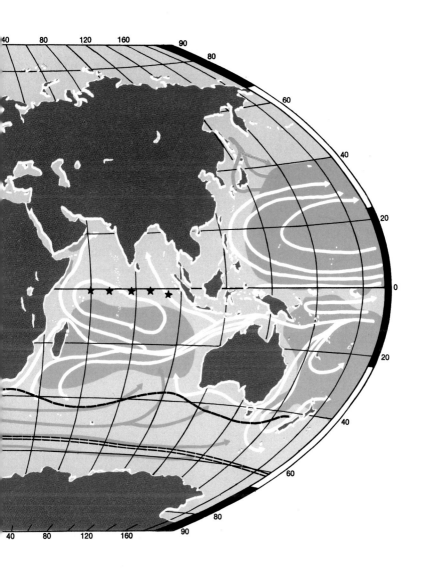

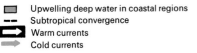
Upwelling deep water in coastal regions
Subtropical convergence
Warm currents
Cold currents

Light

Illumination is a very important factor in the life of the
organisms that are the basis of the food chain. Depending on
the clearness of the water, plant life disappears between 150
and 200 metres, and the animals that feed on vegetation are
also lacking at this depth. Even at considerable depths there is
plant and animal plankton, brought by the currents. Sunlight
almost disappears at 750 metres. The band of weakly lit waters
is called the photic zone; the aphotic zone is where there is no
sunlight. But even in the aphotic zone there is some luminosity
because of the luminous organisms or bacteria. In the sea's two
further zones can be distinguished, the pelagic and benthic
environments, the latter subdivided in turn into a littoral
region and a deep-sea one. These are useful divisions for
determining the favourite haunts of the various species. In the
open sea, apart from the continental shelf made up of the
submerged edge of the continental land mass, there is a pelagic
region between the surface and a depth of 200 metres. It is an
extremely large environment, but only a seventh of the sea's
species live there. Beneath this is the bathypelagic region, from
200 to 3,000 metres. The species living in this zone, which is
physically relatively stable, are almost ten times more varied
than those in the upper zone. Considering the similarity of the
surroundings of all the seas at this depth, it is not difficult to
find cosmopolitan fishes in it. In fact, while a surface fish that
lives in the cold waters north of the Atlantic Ocean will never
be able to reach the waters of the Antarctic, nor adapt to the
temperatures of the tropical seas, a fish of the depths, given the
uniformity of temperature on the ocean-bottom, will have no
difficulty in reaching the waters of the other hemisphere. Many
species of this region carry out conspicuous vertical migrations
in the course of the seasons and also during the course of a day.

Below 3,000 metres is the abysso-pelagic region and the
region of the great oceanic trenches. At these depths reduced
forms of life predominate, which are specialists at living in an
environment poor in food. This is the region of the carnivores
and detritus-eaters, because it is totally lacking in any form of
vegetable life, although there are many invertebrates. The
temperature of the water is always below 4°C. During
exploration of the great marine trenches, fishes have been
caught at depths of up to 7,000 metres (for example,
Grimaldichthys profundissimus and *Careproctus
amblystomopsis*). While diving in the Marianas trench, at the
maximum depth known, the French scientist Piccard claims to
have seen a flatfish at around 10,300 metres. It was more
probably a holothurian, but in any event it was living in a
habitat at which the pressure was greater than 1,000
atmospheres, equal to a ton per square centimetre of surface.
Animals that live at great depths and in constant contact with
the bottom can be called bathybenthonic. This region is

particularly rich in sediment and organic detritus, and is covered with thousands of millions of minute skeletons of invertebrates, in particular radiolarians, which have siliceous skeletons; up to 3,700 metres the calcareous skeletons of foraminferans, and above all globigerinas, predominate. The neritic zone, which begins on the shore-line and covers the whole of the continental shelf, is very different. It can be very extended, as on the Newfoundland banks, or almost non-existent, as in the Ligurian Sea. Its special feature is its variations in temperature and salinity and the greater or lesser influence of dry land on the supply of fresh water and mineral salts. The presence of light favours the growth of submerged vegetation and phytoplankton. This zone has a very varied fauna, with populations that often take on local characteristics; brackish zones are also linked with it.

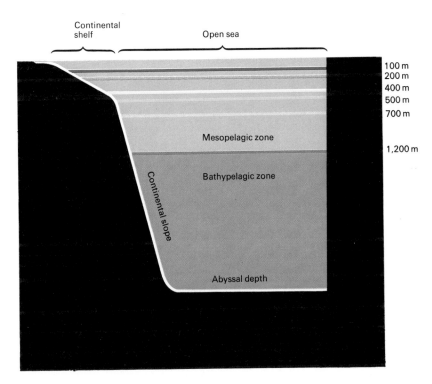

Pelagic fishes

The sea is the kingdom of the rapid, tireless swimmers. The prevalent body shape is fusiform, which offers the least friction to the liquid element; the colour is almost uniformly blue-grey, and the body counter-shaded; both predator and prey employ the same weapons: speed and invisibility. Underwater divers who have seen large sharks or a barracuda, have been struck by the sudden appearance of these predators. They rise out of nowhere, like ghosts, and rapidly launch an attack or disappear. Sharks are the subject of many bloodthirsty true stories; certainly many large, warm-water sharks are potential man-eaters. Most dangerous are the members of the family Isuridae, which include well-known species such as the white shark (*Carcharodon carcharias*; see ill. on p. 189), the principal man-eater. One detail makes the Isuridae immediately recognisable from other sharks: their tail, which is markedly asymmetrical in the majority of cartilaginous fishes, has two almost equal lobes. This makes them more like tunnies than sharks, because they also have keels on both sides of the caudal peduncle, which help to make their swimming more powerful. Their jaws, which are equipped with very pointed, triangular teeth that are slightly serrated in the white shark, are capable of swallowing fairly large prey. This, together with the fact that sharks are in the habit of tasting anything that seems edible, leads them to attack small boats and animals which have accidentally fallen into the sea. Seals, dogs, other sharks, and remains of all kinds such as tins, bottles, etc., have been found in the stomachs of white sharks. The white shark lives in the open sea, but in certain conditions it can be seen near beaches. Its danger diminishes when it is in colder waters than usual, but because it lives in temperate and tropical waters, it should always be considered dangerous. The largest example ever caught measured 6·4 metres, while the average maximum is around five metres, with a weight which can exceed three tons.

▼ White tunny
Thunnus alalunga

Dolphin fish ▶
Coryphaena hippurus

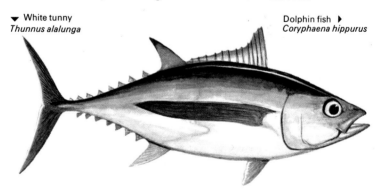

▲ White marlin
Tetrapterus albidus

These sharks live near the surface for preference, but one has been caught over a thousand metres down. Even if it is smaller and less dangerous, the mako (*Isurus oxyrinchus*) should not be underrated. It lives in the Atlantic and the Mediterranean. The same species (usually known as the blue pointer) lives in the seas of India, Australia, and in the Pacific Ocean. It usually weighs less than half a ton and is not more than three and a half metres long, but its agility and speed make it fearful. Its capture is spectacular. Common in the Atlantic Ocean and the Mediterranean, including Italian seas, is the porbeagle (*Lamna nasus*), which, like the mako, is caught for its flesh, which is highly valued in some parts.

Easily recognisable by their very asymmetrical tail, the thresher shark (*Alopias vulpinus*) is a fast swimmer which is extremely voracious but not harmful to man. The upper lobe of the tail is almost the length of their body and in the young is very much longer than the body. The thresher shark is very adept at using it to beat schools of small fishes to force them to scatter so that it can catch them more easily. Because of this habit it is often the victim of fish-hooks lowered for tunnies, which sometimes remain caught in its tail. Thresher sharks live in both tropical and temperate waters, including the Mediterranean and British waters. They are caught along the American coasts of the Pacific Ocean commercially. Even if some of them are six metres long, their weight is always less than half a ton, and a large part of their length is made up of their tail.

▼ Sword fish
Xiphias gladius

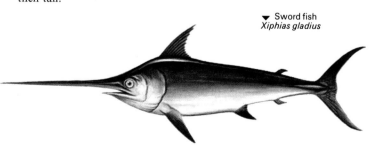

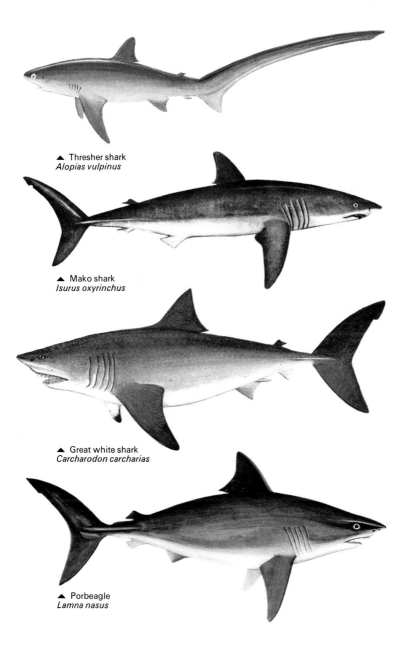

▲ Thresher shark
Alopias vulpinus

▲ Mako shark
Isurus oxyrinchus

▲ Great white shark
Carcharodon carcharias

▲ Porbeagle
Lamna nasus

189

The Carcharinidae, which includes the tiger shark (*Galeocerdo cuvieri*), is a family known for its man-eating habits. As voracious as the white shark, it hardly ever comes near the coast and has never been recorded in the Mediterranean, although it is often found on the African coasts of the Atlantic.

The eagle rays and mantas, cartilaginous fishes famous for their large pectoral fins are also pelagic fishes. The manta, or sea-devil as it is called by some fishermen, arouses terror by its

▼ Eagle rays *Aetobatis narinari*

size. One of the largest examples caught weighed a ton and a half and was more than six metres long. Although this gigantic animal has a peaceful nature and is not interested in man, the immense force of its wings makes them best avoided. Sometimes giants have been seen to jump out of the water and fall on the surface with an impressive roar. It has been suggested that this manoeuvre helps the fish to free itself from parasites and perhaps to give birth. The mantas are plankton-feeders and feed by means of 'horns' at the side of the mouth to

▲ Opah
Lampris guttatus

Hammerhead shark
Sphyrna zygaena ▶

funnel in the food which they collect while swimming with their
mouths open. Most rays lead a bottom-living life, but in some
cases, such as in *Aetobatus* and *Rhinoptera*, they do not disdain
life in the open sea. These species come near the coasts in the
breeding period, but are found throughout the tropical
Atlantic at other periods. The Aetobatidae, like the
Myliobatidae, eat a large amount of oysters and other shellfish
and cause serious damage to the cultivation of these molluscs,
so much so that in America the oyster beds are protected with
strong fences. Sting-rays and some mantas are equipped with
long stings with venom tissue that are also dangerous to man:
abdominal wounds can, in fact, be fatal.

Bony fishes which lead pelagic lives are fine swimmers and
have a fusiform body as a common characteristic. In

comparison with sharks which, apart from the white shark, the mako, and the thresher shark, are rather slow in their movements, the bony fishes are much faster and more manoeuvrable. Tunnies and marlins are the top speed contenders; both are capable of reaching 70 km an hour. Moreover, unlike the sharks, they can brake their speed abruptly, immediately falling on their prey. In general the pelagic bony fishes are fairly large or large, ranging from bonitos of just over half a metre to huge marlins weighing more than half a ton and more than three metres long, and swordfishes of even greater dimensions. There are also tunnies in shallower waters, but only adjacent to the deep sea, and in these zones they are subject to more intensive fishing. Tunnies and other fast pelagic fishes, as well as the more active species of sharks, have a higher body temperature than the water; a network of veins under the skin helps them maintain their body heat. Because their metabolic reactions are more rapid the body temperature increases within certain limits, and such fishes are probably much faster because they have a higher level of muscular efficiency than fishes whose temperature is equal to that of their surroundings. Then there are some pipe-fishes and the frog-fish that live in the Sargasso weed, the branching algae of the sea of the same name, and which look very like the yellowish-brown algae. The Lampridiformes, which include

▼ Bonito
Sarda sarda

species such as the opah (*Lampris guttatus*; see ill. on p. 192) which has a respectable weight of two and a half tons and excellent flesh, have the fewest species of all oceanic families in the tropical and temperate seas.

The oarfish (*Regalecus glesne*), which is more than six metres long, and the ribbon-fish (*Trachipterus*), which is about three metres long, both have a ribbon-like appearance. They are rarely caught, and so are of only limited interest.

▼ Oarfish *Regalecus glesne*

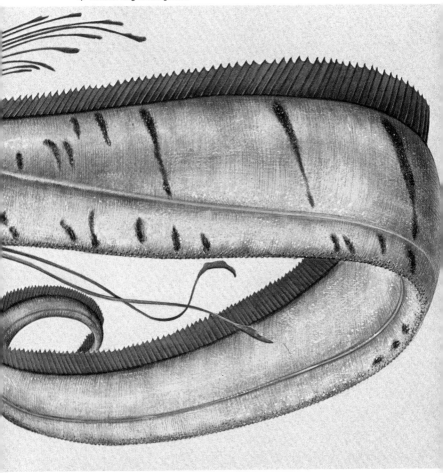

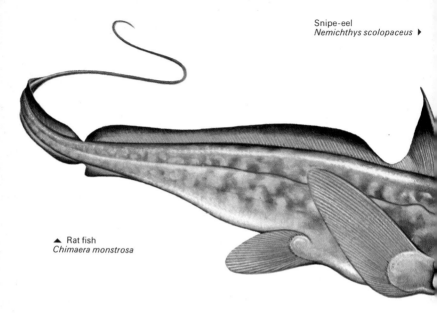

Snipe-eel
Nemichthys scolopaceus ▶

▲ Rat fish
Chimaera monstrosa

Deep-water fishes

The fauna of the deep sea is particularly rich in species, but
they are less numerous than those of the pelagic region. The
dimensions of these animals, who are adapted to such extreme
conditions, are rather small. Apart from the giants of the
marine depths, such as the members of the family
Alepisauridae, which are just under two metres, the average
length is about 20–30 cm. Besides their small size, deep-water
fishes have a delicate, diaphanous appearance that contrasts
with the enormous pressure they support. Each square
centimetre of their body surface is subject to great pressure that
does not crush the animal because it is counterbalanced by the
pressure inside the fish. The diaphanous appearance and
limited dimensions reflect the calm of the bottom of the sea and
the difficulty bigger forms have in finding food. The capture of
food is, in fact, the major problem of deep sea fishes. There are
many solutions, some rather surprising. Teeth are often long,
pointed, and set in a mouth with a considerable gape. The
mouths of some of these fishes can open wide enough to admit
fish almost as large as the predator itself. The digestive organs
are also adapted: they can dilate and, as in the *Chiasmodon
niger*, extend until they become transparent, so that the
engulfed fish can be seen. The kingdom of the deep sea fishes
extends from a depth of 250 metres to the bottom of the sea, so
that some species live in the photic zone and others in the

196

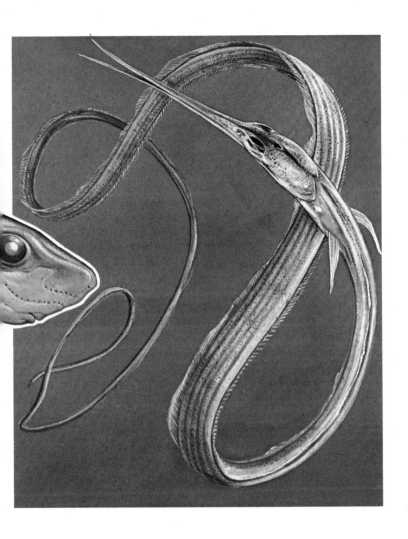

sunless zone. According to the depth, there are considerable differences in the size of eyes in the photic zone, and they gradually disappear little by little as the light decreases to the greatest depths. Even in the sunless zone there is some light. As we have already mentioned, fishes and other deep sea organisms are equipped with photophores, some of which are situated on strange, branching appendages.

197

The hatchet fish (*Argyropelecus hemigymnus*) has an interesting visual adaptation. Its eyes are turned upwards and equipped with an elaborate optical structure that allows them to pick up the weakest light.

Some species rise by night to lesser depths in search of food, but in general the deep sea fishes do not approach the surface. The variation of external pressure on the body cavities containing gas, or liquids with dissolved gases, would cause decompression problems.

▼ *Vinciguerra attenuata*　　　　▼ *Lasiognathus saccostoma*

▲ *Chauliodus sloanei*　　　　▲ *Linophyrne arborifera*

▲ Hatchet fish *Argyropelecus hemigymnus*

The coral reef

Coral environments are found near the equator almost all round the Earth's circumference and are one of the richest and most interesting faunistic assemblages. It is the realm of colour and warm waters, and it is well lit and has a high density of animal population. The density of the fishes on a coral reef is as much as 250 tons a square kilometre and, apart from climatic conditions, it is linked to the productivity of the invertebrates and algae, which ensure the presence of abundant food. The principal species found in this underwater paradise are butterfly-fishes, angel-fishes, wrasses, trigger-fishes and surgeon-fishes. Among the predators there are plenty of morays, needle-fishes, sharks, barracudas, groupers, and jacks. Surgeon-fishes are a group of bony fishes that lead a vegetarian life on the coral reef. Their name derives not from any activity but from the fact that the caudal peduncle has a very flexible bony blade that looks rather like a kind of surgical knife. Their mouth is well adapted to browse the encrusting algae from the calcareous skeleton of the coral polyps. Some blennies, butterfly-fishes, and gobies are also herbivorous or mainly herbivorous. Then there are the coral eaters, which also usually feed on crustaceans and molluscs. Corals are sessile invertebrates with a calcareous support that allows the polyps which form their colonies rise to the outside.

Butterfly-fishes and angel-fishes have rather protruberant mouths equipped with numerous tiny teeth with which they nip the expanded coral polyps. They are among the most beautiful coral fishes. They stand out because of their gaudy colours, and

▼ Coral producing zones   Bottom of a coral reef ▶

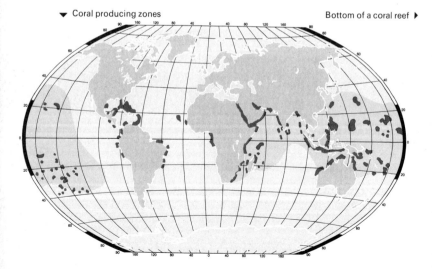

▲ *Chaetodontoplus mesoleucus*

the difference between them is that the angel-fishes have a spine on the lower gill-cover. They are very prized as aquarium fishes, though their breeding calls for special care and controlled feeding. Their splendid colours vary according to the age of the individuals. The young often have lighter, more uniform hues than the adults. The bright colours have an

▼ *Pomacanthus annularis*

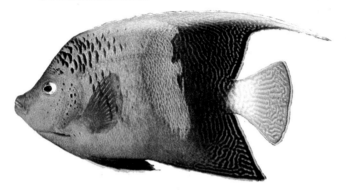

important concealing function in such a colourful environment. In fact, the bands of colour and the marking and shading of these fishes can confuse possible adversaries. Both the butterfly-fishes and the angel-fishes live alone or in small groups which are never large enough to be schools. They never go far away from the coral, the numerous crevices of which offer a refuge from predators.

The Platacidae have very large fins that have given them the name bat-fishes. Their mouth is very similar to that of the butterfly-fishes. They live in the Red Sea and the Indian Ocean where, as they are euryhaline, they are able to penetrate into brackish lagoons.

▼ *Chaetodon ephippium*

Overleaf: Coral reef ▶

Other coral-eating fishes get their food in different ways from those already described. Unlike butterfly-fishes, the trigger-fishes and the parrot fishes, not only attack the sprouting part of the polyps but also eat the calcareous covering. Parrot-fishes also have the strange habit of enclosing themselves in a mucus envelope during the night. The function of this sheath is probably to serve as a defence against nocturnal predators such as morays, which are in the habit of remaining hidden in their lairs all day and going out at night to hunt and as both wrasses and parrot-fishes sleep at night they would be very vulnerable. Another adaptation of these coral-eaters is grinding whole pieces of the coral formation with their teeth. The fish that do

▼ Bat-fish *Platax orbicularis*

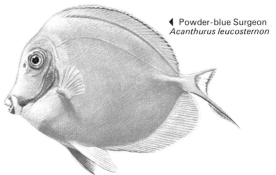

◀ Powder-blue Surgeon
Acanthurus leucosternon

▼ Below: *Acanthurus lineatus*   Bottom: *Chaetodon collaris*

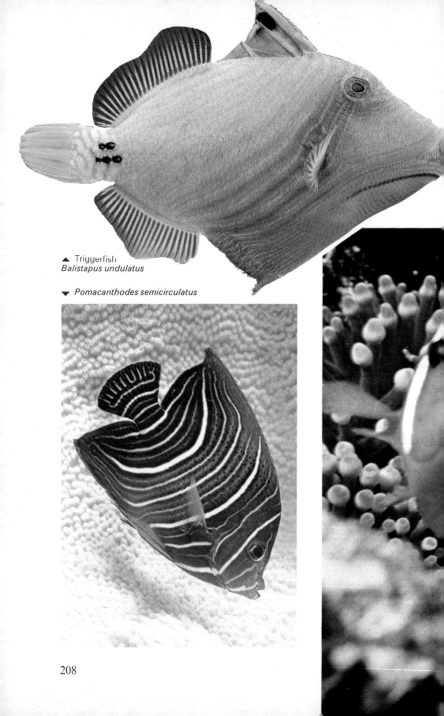

▲ Triggerfish
Balistapus undulatus

▼ *Pomacanthodes semicirculatus*

this have teeth reinforced with strong bony plates that grind up everything, thereby allowing the digestive system to extract the food from the pile of detritus taken in. The amount of actual food obtained by this method is very small, so these fishes are forced to browse on the corals continually to make sure of enough food. The most important representatives of this category are the parrot fishes, the triggerfishes (Balistidae), and the puffer-fishes. A Red Sea species, *Odonus niger*, has red teeth instead of white as is normal in the Balistidae and the majority of fishes. The trigger-fishes have a very hard body surface which is covered with small bony plates instead of the

▼ *Amphiprion ephippium*

usual scales. They also have a first dorsal fin with three, very strong, spine-like rays that can be erected at will and locked into position as a defensive weapon. The puffer-fishes, Tetradontidae are also not without a means of defence; if molested, they are able to swell up into a spine-covered sphere. The porcupine-fish (*Diodon hystrix*) reaches 90 cm in diameter,

▼ *Cephalopholis miniatus*

and when it swells the numerous spines with which it is equipped are erected. Many species of Serranidae, including the well known groupers, live in tropical seas. The tropical serranid, *Cephalopholis*, is distinguished by its reddish colour (above); other species of tropical serranids are highly prized by aquarists for their brilliant colours.

Pelagic fishes are in contact with the coral world only while on short sorties in search of prey. The richness of the plankton also attracts plankton-feeding fish.

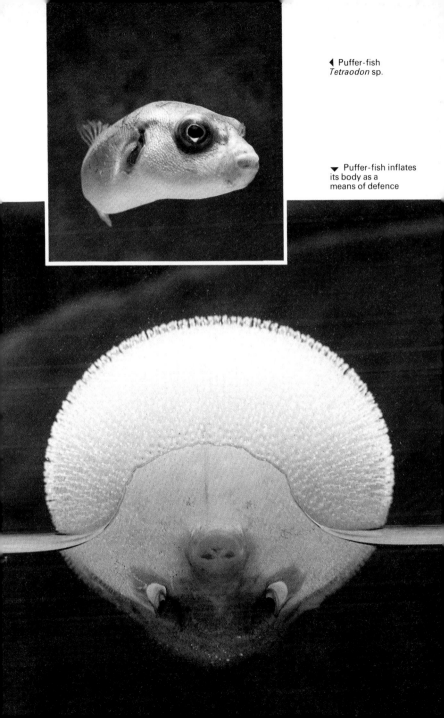

◀ Puffer-fish
Tetraodon sp.

▼ Puffer-fish inflates
its body as a
means of defence

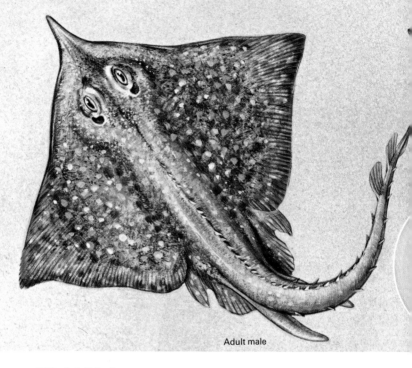

Adult male

▲ White skate *Raja alba*

Mediterranean fishes

The Mediterranean has very varied characteristics. Its
maximum depth of 4,600 metres permits the presence of deep
sea fishes and a conspicuous pelagic and above all neritic
fauna, which is found on the continental shelf around the
Italian coasts, in the Adriatic Sea, and close to the African
coasts. The average salinity of 37 parts per thousand rises near
the eastern coasts, while it is lower in the Adriatic and near the
mouths of rivers; typical are the brackish environments of
lagoons and estuaries, with a small number of species but many
individuals.

The Mediterranean can be considered to be a temperate sea,
given that its temperature varies from 12–13°C in winter and

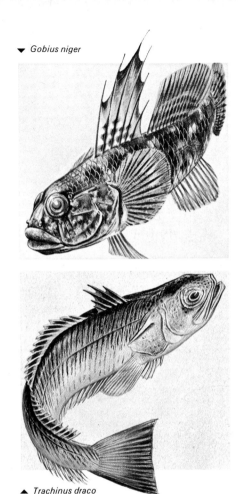

▼ *Gobius niger*

juvenile

egg-case

▲ *Trachinus draco*

20–25°C in summer. In this all the species are littoral or neritic, with the exception of a few deep-sea fauna. Many species are endemic: cartilaginous fishes include the rays, which are eaten in certain areas. The Gobiidae are also endemic, with many marine and brackish species. Typical of the Venetian lagoon is *Gobius niger,* the black goby, and the rock goby (*Gobius paganellus*), which lives in lairs hollowed out under stones even in zones which are sometimes uncovered by the low tide. The weever-fish (*Trachinus*) is affected by seasonal changes; in the warm months it is found on sandy beaches and muddy estuaries, buried at the bottom, with its dorsal fin, which is armed with venomous spines, erected; in winter, it moves towards deeper zones (around 100 metres). The Mullidae and

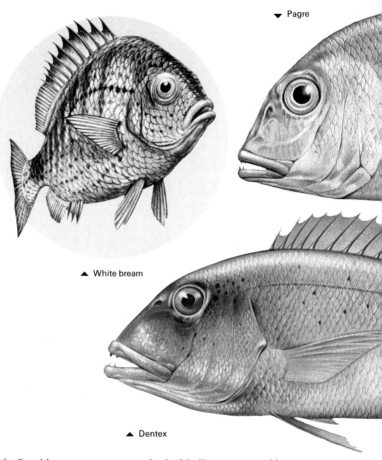

▼ Pagre

▲ White bream

▲ Dentex

the Sparidae are very common in the Mediterranean and in Italian waters, and are prized as food. Well known Mullidae are the red mullets (*Mullus surmuletus* and *M. barbatus*), which changes colour when they die. Of the sea breams (Sparidae), the dentex and the pagre can be as much as a metre long and weigh ten kilogrammes. They are very similar in shape, but have different colours: dentex (*Dentex dentex*) is silver-blue with spots and the pagre (*Pagrus pagrus*) pink or red. The dentex is common on shallow, sandy bottoms with plenty of vegetation; the pagre prefers sandy, muddy bottoms up to 200 metres. The white bream (*Diplodus sargus*; in the circle) is a sea bream with coastal habits and is very common

and easy to see among the rocks. Its flesh is less sought after than that of its fellows, but it is eaten in certain areas. Much prized is the gilthead (*Sparus auratus*; see ill. on p. 217), which lives either on a stony bottom near the shore or on submerged vegetation. It is also found on sandy bottoms and, as it is euryhaline, in lagoons and estuaries. It reaches a weight of five kilogrammes and a length of seventy centimetres, is typical of the northern Adriatic, and is found commonly near the coasts of Yugoslavia, where it is often caught. The bogue (*Boops boops*; below) is an omnivorous fish found all year round on the coast, where it is frequently seen. It can be caught in various ways, even with a line. The young of this species have a protective, symbiotic relationship with some jellyfishes, whose tentacles can inflict stings which are painful to man and fatal to the majority of fishes. The saddled bream (*Oblada melanura*), recognisable by the black spot on its caudal peduncle, is very similar. Several species of the family Serranidae live in the Mediterranean, with a preference for rocky bottoms. The dusty bream, *Epinepheius guaza* is one of the prey most sought by underwater hunters. It is equipped with spines on its back and gill covers. When speared in its lair, it bends itself and cannot be withdrawn until it is dead. The young dusky perch live near the surface, preferably under floating wreckage. The flesh of sea perches is good, but gourmets prefer another related species, the bass (*Dicentrarchus labrax*; see ill. on p. 221), whose flesh is tastier. It lives all over the Mediterranean, wherever the bottom is sandy, is common in lagoons and, because it is euryhaline, also in rivers.

The grey mullet family Mugilidae live in the waters of the Mediterranean, with a particular preference for those rich in all kinds of detritus, the favourite food of these omnivorous fishes, which are euryhaline to the considerable degree. They are common in all surroundings where organic material of an earthly nature is found, and they also make their way into shallow, heavily polluted waters. They are numerous in ports and river estuaries, which they travel a long way up. Their flesh is usually prized, but it can easily become impregnated with hydrocarbons without the fish apparently suffering. This can

▼ Bogue

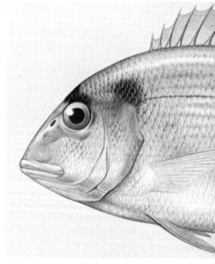

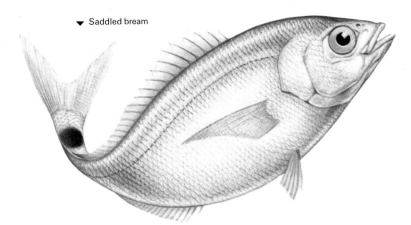

▼ Saddled bream

easily happen in polluted waters, making it inedible. They are intensively fished with a kind of dragnet that is used in canals and along the mouths of Adriatic rivers.

Among the pelagic fishes in the Mediterranean we must not forget the sardine or pilchard, which is the object of intensive commercial fishing. Mediterranean sardines are not as big as the Atlantic ones, perhaps as a result of their shorter lives. The gilt sardine (*Sardinella aurita*) and the sprat (*Sprattus sprattus*)

▼ Gilthead

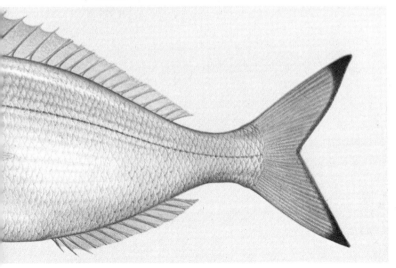

217

▲ John Dory *Zeus faber*

are also important. The sprat was also called 'Papalina' by
Adriatic fishermen of the papal territories, a name still used in
the Venice. The eggs of these fishes are spherical, unlike those
of anchovies, which are elliptical. The anchovy and the sardine
are equally important for fishing and for the production of
whitebait, the fry of both species, which are a gastronomic
delicacy. The tunny and the swordfish are two large bony fishes
common in the Mediterranean. The tunny is very important
and is caught with special equipment in Sicily and Sardinia. In
addition to the blue-fin tunny, the albacore (*Thunnus alalunga*),
a smaller fish with long fins, is found in the Mediterranean. The
flesh of the swordfish is also prized. It is preferably fished near

▲ Shore rockling *Gaidopsarus mediterraneus*

the Strait of Messina, in summer, when it is approaching the coasts for reproduction. Few members of the cod family, the Gadidae are present in the Mediterranean, but the shore rockling (*Gaidropsarus mediterranean*) is found there. The hake lives at depths of over 100 metres, while the rockling is to be seen in shallow waters, where there are beds of algae. The John Dory (*Zeus faber*; see ill. on p. 218), lives in deep waters and is much prized for its flesh. The angler-fish, an ugly looking bottom-living fish with very tasty flesh, is found in the same surroundings. Many species of flat-fish, all edible and prized, are caught in the Mediterranean, on sandy or muddy bottoms, at depths of a few metres to more than 200 metres.

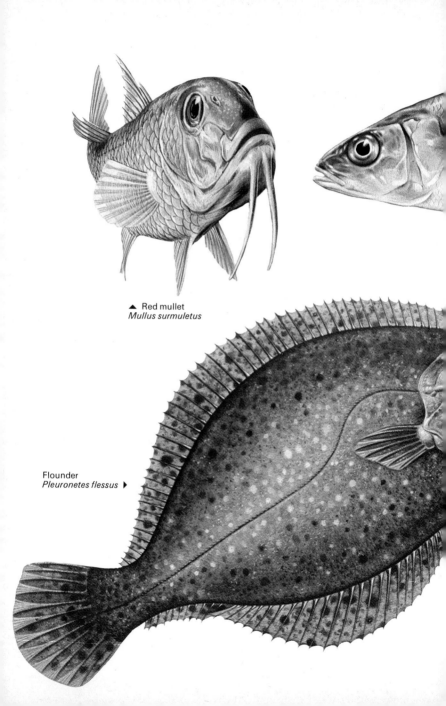

▲ Red mullet
Mullus surmuletus

Flounder
Pleuronetes flessus ▶

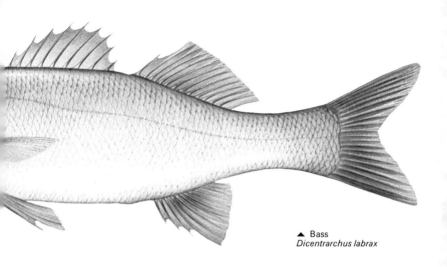

▲ Bass
Dicentrarchus labrax

Fishes of the polar seas
The greatest problem of fishes that live in very cold
surroundings is how to maintain activity at a temperature very
near to blood freezing point. Polar fishes are very active at a
temperature of −2°C, and their metabolism is perfectly able to
carry out all its functions. The behaviour of polar fishes
contrasts with the tendency of warm-water fishes to reduce
their activity when the temperature goes down and to have a
lower growth rate during winter. Even more interesting is the
study carried out on some Labrador fishes whose blood freezes
at −1°C, while the temperature of the water stays constantly at
−1 75°C. The blood of these fishes is in an unstable condition
called super-cooled. Super-cooled liquids remain in a liquid
state at temperatures lower than those of solidification, but a
slight shock or contact with an ice crystal is enough to cause all
the liquid rapidly to solidify. In fact some temperate-water
fishes can survive in super-cooled waters at −3°C, but contact
with an ice cube would be enough to kill them. It seems that
their blood contains an organic antifreeze that enables them to
survive in extreme conditions. The fish fauna of the Antarctic
ocean consists mainly of the fishes of the family Nototheniidae.
There are also rays, eel-pouts (Zoarcidae), and sea-snails
(Liparidae). There are no nototheniids in Arctic seas, but there
are Zoarcidae, Liparidae, Gadidae, and flat-fishes. The
Chaenichthyidae are particularly interesting Antarctic fishes;
they have so few red blood cells that they are called bloodless
fish. But despite their lack of red globules, they breathe
normally in well-oxygenated, cold water. The oxygen is carried
in solution in the plasma.

221

Trematomus pennellii

Chaenodraco wilsoni

Lycodes seminudus

Myxocephalus scorpius

Freshwater fishes

Fresh waters have a salt content of less than 0·5 % and are also subject to considerable variation. The temperature of lakes which may vary from top to bottom because of shallowness, is influenced by sunlight and the temperature of their tributaries. Moreover, the surface can freeze in winter, while in summer the water can be reduced or even disappear. The water in lakes is usually fairly calm, and it is stagnant in pools and marshes. The running waters of torrents and rivers can reach considerable speed. Where running waters are converted into enclosed or stagnant waters by a dam in the river, the change is usually accompanied by a change in fauna. Alpine streams, whose

▼ Food chains in a lake

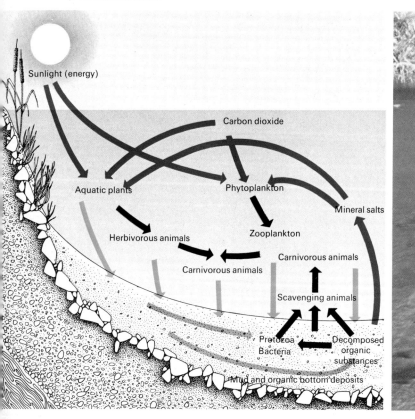

cold, fast-running waters are very well oxygenated, are inhabited by stenothermic species which need high oxygen levels. Such individuals are able to swim against the currents, a typical example being the salmon. In the lower reaches of the rivers, or in areas where the river-bed widens, eurythermic fishes are found. The slowless and shallowness of these waters leads to them becoming warm and the plants in it prevent the dissolved oxygen from diminishing. These waters are inhabited by slow-water fishes with stout bodies such as the barbel (*Barbus barbus*), the carp (*Cyprinus carpio*), and the chub (*Leuciscus cephalus*). Species from other, far distant areas have been successfully introduced into fresh waters. The American

▼ Plants and animals of a lake

▲ Grayling   ▲ *Gambusia*

rainbow trout (*Salmo gardneri*) was introduced into Europe at the end of the last century and is found abundantly in Italy. A small cyprinodont, *Gambusia affinis*, that feeds mainly on larvae of the mosquito, has been introduced into Italy to combat malaria. Other freshwater fishes are adapted versions of marine species. The burbot (*Lota lota*), for example, belongs to the same family as the cod (Gadidae), and lives in European fresh waters and reproduces with submerged eggs, unlike its

▼ Barbel

American rainbow trout   Bleak ▶

▼ Burbot *Lota lota*

▼ Burbot *Lota lota*

marine relatives, which lay floating eggs. It is very prolific (it lays as many as a million eggs), usually measures 70–80 cm and can be as long as a metre in the waters around Siberia.

Freshwater fishes that merit particular attention are the sturgeons (family Acipenseridae). Well-known for their eggs which are a great delicacy (caviar), they are also important for characteristics which are unique amongst bony fishes. The shape of sturgeons is very like that of sharks. They have no

▼ Sturgeon *Acipenser sturio*

scales but five rows of bony plates. They have sensitive barbels on their snout which are used to search for food. Being freshwater fishes, most of their time in the sea is spent searching for food such as molluscs, crustaceans and tiny fishes. Sturgeons move very slowly and their major preoccupation is catching food. They can survive in captivity for many weeks without any food. They are also very large, the beluga (*Huso huso*) is the largest at almost four metres long and

weighs a ton. Reproduction takes place in fresh water, and the breeding fish ascend the rivers in the same way as salmon. The sturgeon has a very long life: it certainly exceeds seventy-five years and may perhaps reach a century. It reaches sexual maturity around twenty. The slowness of their reproductive cycle and the intensive fishing to which they are subjected has in many places endangered their survival.

As in the sea, the freshwater food chain depends on phytoplankton and submerged vegetation which capture solar energy. Given the usual shallowness of fresh waters, all the environments (rivers, lakes, etc.) are enriched in this way. The exceptions are the very deep lakes, such as Lake Baikal, which has a maximum depth of 1,741 metres and contains numerous endemic cottoid fishes which go down to depths of more than 1,000 metres in the cold months. In this lake, as in the sea, there is a photic and a sunless zone, and the temperature is constant under the surface layers. The majority of inland waters have an average depth of not more than 10 metres. If shallowness favours isolation and therefore the production of

◀ Platy *Xiphorphorus maculatus*   ▼ Piranha *Serrasalmus*

231

phytoplankton and vegetable organisms, the currents typical of many fresh waters disperse the plankton, which does well only where the waters are calmer, as in lakes and river mouths. Many terrestrial species such as insects and annelids also contribute to the freshwater food chain. At the top of the food chain are carnivores such as the pike and the trout, which not only prey on other fishes but also on amphibians, small mammals and birds. The piranha (*Serrasalmus piraya*; see p. 231) is the best-known freshwater carnivore, but the stories told about it are often the products of fantasy. The fish lives in shoals in the rivers of South America, above all in Brazil or in the tributaries of the Rio San Francesco where they say that a cow can be completely stripped in less than five minutes. The piranha mouth is actually equipped with strong jaws armed with very sharp, triangular teeth, but their aggressiveness seems to be directed only towards other fishes or animals in difficulty. However, the attack by a school of them is considered dangerous even for man, as the shoals contain more than a hundred individuals and perhaps even as many as a thousand.

▼ Glass catfish
Keyptopterus bicirrhis

Angel fish
Pterophyllum scalare ▶

▲ Neon tetra *Hyphessobrycon innesi*

▼ Snake-head *Channa asiatica*

Aquarium fishes

Many freshwater and marine species have become very well known through their cultivation as aquarium animals. A cyprinid native to Asia and known all over the world, is the goldfish; it can stand up to the most unfavourable conditions. Breeding and cross-breeding have produced a species that has many varieties with very long fins, strange eyes, and a variety of colours. Another greatly admired aquarium species is the neon tetra (*Hyphessobrycon innesi*; photo on the left) which, because of its splendid red and blue reflections, gives the impression of being lit up.

The cost of setting up a tropical marine aquarium is certainly more expensive than a freshwater aquarium but watching the non-stop activity of the marine coral-reef fishes with their unbelievable colours is very rewarding and impressive. Invertebrates such as bright sea snails and sea anemones can be kept in the same tank.

▼ Green puffer-fish *Tetraodon fluviatilis*

Cave fishes

Subterranean waters are the habitat of various aquatic animals which have adapted to living in conditions of almost total darkness. The waters in caves form rivers, lakes or even small pools of water, in which fishes may live. The temperature of these underground waters is almost constant and is the same or a little lower than the surrounding air. Plant-life which needs light to live is very scarce or non-existent. As we have seen, plants are the basis of every food chain, however, and in their absence the cave fishes are only able to live because the water from outside brings vegetable remains and organic detritus left by surface animals. A large group of invertebrates draws the necessary food from these sources. Numerous crustaceans, many of them planktonic, live in the underground waters, especially in the quietest zones. These form part of an aquatic food chain and become the prey of fishes.

The lack of light has evolved species that, like the bottom-dwelling fishes, have no eyes or very reduced optic organs, and the corresponding optic centres of the brain are also reduced. These fishes, though incapable of seeing, are able to catch prey through the refinement of other sensory organs. The lateral line, the olfactory organs, and the nerve endings are better developed in cave fishes than in others, so that they are perfectly capable of moving about in their surroundings without vision.

The Amblyopsidae are a family of blind fishes that live in North American fresh waters, in surroundings of the same geological origin. They live in the underground waters of caves formed of calcareous rocks produced in the Cretaceous Period. They are small fishes, whitish because of their lack of pigment, and if they are kept in a lighted aquarium, after about three months they will develop weak pigment. One of these amblyopsids, that has rudimentary eyes, can go on moving agilely and feeding itself even if its eyes are removed.

Other cave fishes are *Caecobarbus*, and *Anoptichthys jordani* (in the ill. on the facing page), which may have evolved, through adaptation to surroundings without light, from *Astyanax mexicanus*, a fish with functional eyes. The eyes of *Anoptichthys* and *Caecobarbus* are reduced during growth and become covered with skin; but they retain part of the sensitivity, to the extent that they move away from light. The majority of fishes without eyes are very active: they are always on the move and explore their surroundings with a zig-zag movement. This may be a way of compensating for their lack of sight, for by continually exploring the space around them, they increase the possibilities of finding food.

Blind cave fish (inset)
in its natural environment ▶

Fishes and Man

An important source of food

Since his appearance on Earth, man has devoted his life to an increasingly frantic search for food, a search the consequences of which are particularly felt in various areas of the world where there has been drastic reductions in local fauna. The sea, however, gives hope for the future as a good source of food for a popular approaching nearer to the limits the Earth can support. Some species of fishes, both marine and freshwater, have been successfully bred in fisheries or in artificial reservoirs and natural lakes. In rice-fields for example, the growing of rice is combined with the breeding of freshwater fishes such as cyprinids and cichlids. Carps and *Tilapia*, which are very prolific, could provide an important source of food in the future.

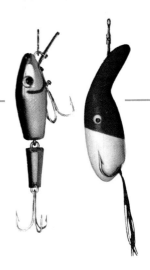

Fishing

The growth of fish-culture may help solve the problem of food shortage, but at the same time fishing will have to be increased and controlled. Until now, apart from sporadic attempts at control, it has been carried on in an indiscriminate way. For the sea, in spite of fishing and pollution, has shown itself to be one of the environments best able to support man. If the vast areas of salt water were properly exploited, we could extract twice as much fish, and therefore protein, as we do. Moreover, by the controlled rearing of young fishes which could then be set free in their natural surroundings, we could considerably increase species with a high food value for man. An experiment like this has been successfully tried with salmon and related species,

239

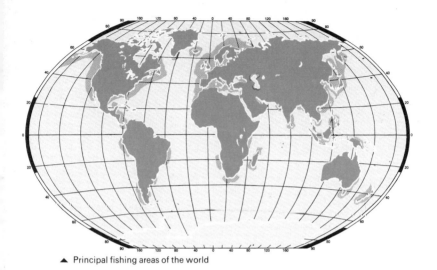

▲ Principal fishing areas of the world

▼ Fishermen on Mauritius

whose fertile eggs can be transported to any part of the world without being damaged. Many salmonids have been imported to Europe from America and have prospered in surroundings very different from their origins, adapting themselves to living always in fresh waters.

Some fishing is done everywhere, but certain areas are particularly important, where the majority of fish consumed fresh are caught or where canning industries have sprung up. The map opposite shows the principal fishing zones, which correspond to the areas of the continental shelf which are rich in food for fishes. Among them is the famous Newfoundland Bank, which represents a fundamental source of cod, herring, and salmon which is exploited in competition by fishermen of many countries. Five countries share more than 50 % of the fish caught. In first place (in 1971) was Peru, with more than ten million tons, a large part of which was made up of Peruvian anchovies which are used both as food and to make fish meal which is used as fertiliser. In second place, with just under ten million tons, was Japan, one of the countries more recently attracted by oceanic fishing and which also occupies a high

▼ 'Trabucco' in use in the Adriatic

▲ A catch of swordfish

position in the cultivation and fishing of crustaceans and molluscs. In third and fourth position were, respectively, China and Russia, with more than seven million tons each. Then came Norway (three million) and the United States (more than two and a half million). Methods of fishing tend to vary, both as a result of local customs and of particular conditions. The net is undoubtedly the most widely used instrument, and there are many variations. The trawl, which hugs the bottom even at considerable depths such as 800 to 1,000 metres, is used industrially. It catches bottom-living fishes, such as plaice and soles, but may in places have the serious drawback that it destroys the vegetation and a large part of the sessile invertebrates, thus impoverishing the area. For this reason, trawling is strictly

▲ Dragging tunny from the net

regulated in certain areas. Fishing with a drift-net held at the front of a boat is widespread, and is particularly used for herrings and anchovies. Industrial fishing is also carried out with fish-hooks, like that done by many Portuguese fishermen, who let down lines with four or five hundred hooks attached. The Japanese have developed a method of fishing with boats that uses a cable up to 15 kilometres long to which an impressive number of hooks is attached.

Traditional fishing survives in many areas with some picturesque local methods. An example is the harpooning of the swordfish, which is carried out in Sicily on board special boats equipped with a mast more than thirty metres high, on which is placed a crows-nest, from which the look-out directs

243

▲ Fishing with a trawl

the boat towards the animal. Characteristic are the capture and slaughter of tunnies with a trap of nets which is practised in the Mediterranean. The capture of the prey takes place amid boiling foam and blood in the so-called death room, where the tunnies collect before being dragged into the boat with gaffs. Typical of some Italian estuaries are the huge lift-nets supported by arms linked to a winch that raises and lowers them. They are used mainly for catching eels and mullets, but they also catch cuttlefish and all the fishes round about. Nor should underwater fishing be forgotten, for it has made a considerable contribution to our knowledge of little-known aspects of underwater life and, with the perfecting of its

Packing and preserving the catch ▲

equipment, it will perhaps contribute to the field of breeding fish in their natural surroundings. Closely connected to large-scale fishing is the kind of industry able to process the fish caught. This is obviously a preserving industry, and it is an important development in some countries. Cod dried in the sun, for example, is one of Norway's most flourishing industries, and it produces a foodstuff that can be kept a long time and stands up to being transported long distances. Also the preserving industry that produces frozen, salted, smoked or tinned salmon is an important development in Canada. There are also specially equipped ships that process fish as soon as it is caught.

Overleaf: Skin diver encounters a moray eel

The classification of fishes

The first attempts to arrange in order the large number of animal species then living took place in the time of Aristotle, who made the first major distinction between animals with blood and those without it. Before Aristotle, animals had had only a group name that placed them according to their salient characteristics as birds (that fly), worms (that crawl), and fishes (that swim), names which do not have any precise zoological definition. Aristotle placed insects, crustaceans and molluscs under animals without blood; those with blood were the viviparous and oviparous quadrupeds, birds, and fishes. Aristotle's animals with blood correspond to the vertebrates of today, while the invertebrates were those without blood. Although limited by lack of knowledge, the Aristotelian division was a good beginning to zoological classification. In fact neither the Romans nor medieval students made any further contribution to a systematic knowledge of animals, because they confined

themselves to describing them and to inventing artificial groupings, dividing animals, for example, into terrestrial, aquatic and flying.

We had to wait until the eighteenth century for anything new in the classification of animals, when Linnaeus introduced the system of binomial nomenclature still used today and a much wilder distinction of zoological groups. But in many ways the empirical division of Aristotle was still not superceded. It was the contributions of Buffon, Cuvier, Lamarck and Darwin that produced a more modern concept from which the modern system is derived; this bases its divisions on the evolution of the species in time and on the position of its components today on the evolutionary ladder. The modern system subdivides the members of the animal kingdom into various groups as follows: the phylum, the class, the order, the family, the genus, and the species.

Under these systematic categories we can classify fishes in the vertebrate phylum and in two classes: cartilaginous fishes and bony fishes. These two classes were formerly united in the superclass Pisces (now the Gnathostomata). This superclass includes the orders, families, genera, and species subdivided on the basis of their origin and evolution. The table opposite is a plan of the classification of fishes showing the classes, subclasses and orders.

Today the fish superclass consists of about 25,000 species out of an animal world of about 1,300,000 species. Of this the insects comprise about a million species, while all the vertebrates, including fishes, amount to about 50,000, a figure which may seem very disproportionate. But we must take into account the fact that the vertebrates are a fairly young group and that certain classes, such as fishes, have hardly passed the initial phase and are still developing. In comparison, invertebrates developed long ago and have had a more complex evolution.

Since the appearance of life on Earth, nature has fought a hard battle for the conquest of the world and has explored many avenues in its attempt to find the best solution. Many of these solutions are now extinct, overtaken by natural selection or more evolved forms. We have only to think of the huge reptiles that peopled the Earth in the Mesozoic Era and disappeared without trace by the end of the Cretaceous, or of the trilobites, which appeared in the Cambrian Period and after a rapid expansion diminished and disappeared in the Permian Period. When the first terrestrial vertebrates appeared, the invertebrates dominated dry land with an impressive number of insects, worms and arachnids. Many of those forms, basically the best adapted, still survive, while others continue as living fossils and are probably the remains of a much larger population from other geological epochs. Classification takes account of all these developments in the re-creation of a genealogical tree, which is useful for dividing the phyla according to criteria that are not purely artificial but reflect actual evolutionary events. There are considerable difficulties in working out the evolutionary position of the phyla because so many of the past connecting links are missing. We know, for example, that the tetrapods or terrestrial vertebrates originated from the Rhipidistia, but the stages of this passage from the water to the land are not known. Almost certainly the species that gradually evolved by acquiring functions adapted to terrestrial life were less inured to hardship than their final forms, by which they were quickly destroyed. This is one reason why systematic groupings are rather tentative. In many cases the lack of deeper knowledge of some group leads to mistakes in their placing. In some cases, however, transitional forms still survive, such as the onychophores, which have been defined as transitional forms between the annelids (segmented worms) and the arthropods (crustaceans, arachnids and insects).

ass	Subclass	Order

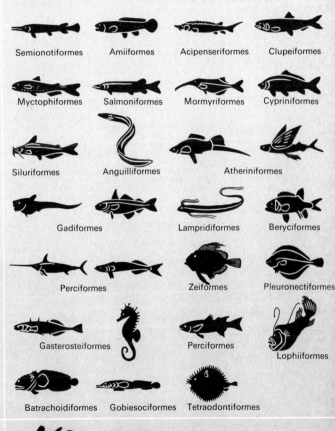

fishes

CHONDRICHTHYES

Lamniformes   Rajiformes   Chimaeriformes

OSTEICHTHYES
(BRANCHIOPTERYGII)

Polypteriformes

Bony fishes

(ACTINOPTERYGI)

Semionotiformes   Amiiformes   Acipenseriformes   Clupeiformes

Myctophiformes   Salmoniformes   Mormyriformes   Cypriniformes

Siluriformes   Anguilliformes   Atheriniformes

Gadiformes   Lampridiformes   Beryciformes

Perciformes   Zeiformes   Pleuronectiformes

Gasterosteiformes   Perciformes   Lophiiformes

Batrachoidiformes   Gobiesociformes   Tetraodontiformes

(CROSSOPTERYGII)

Coelacanthiformes   Ceratodontiformes

251

Bibliography

Modern general works on fishes

Grassé, P., *Traité de Zoologie XIII: Agnates et Poissons.* Massons, Paris, 1958.

Frank, S., *The Pictorial Encyclopaedia of Fishes.* Hamlyn, London, 1971.

Herald, E. S., *Living Fishes of the World.* Hamish Hamilton, London, 1961.

Lagler, K. F., Bardach, J. E. and Miller, R. R., *Ichthyology: The Study of Fishes.* J. Wiley, New York, 1962.

Marshall, N. B., *The Life of Fishes.* Weidenfeld and Nicolson, London, 1965.

Norman, J. R., *A History of Fishes.* E. Benn, 3rd ed. London, 1975.

Schindler, O., *Guide to Freshwater Fishes.* Thames and Hudson, London, New York, 1975. (Details of Central & Northern European species).

Sterba, G., *Freshwater Fishes of the World.* Studio Vista, London, 1966.

Wheeler, A., *Fishes of the World.* Macmillan, New York, 1975.

Books specially relevant to the European fauna

Mediterranean Region

Bini, G., *Atlante dei Pesci delle coste Italiane.* Mondo Sommerso, Rome 1967–71. 9 volumes. (A well illustrated work on all Italian fishes treating their biology in detail)

Luther, W. and Fiedler, K., *Field Guide to the Mediterranean Seashore.* Collins, London, 1976. (A general introduction to coastal animals—invertebrates and fishes)

Riedl, R., *Fauna and Flora der Adria.* P. Parey, Hamburg and Berlin, 1970. (An excellent account of the plants and animals of the Adriatic)

Tortonese, E., *Leptocardia, Cyclostomata, Selachii. Fauna d'italia.* Vol 2. Calderini, Bologna, 1956.

Tortonese, E., *Osteichthyes (pesci ossei) Part 1. Fauna d'italia.* Vol 10. Calderini, Bologna, 1970.

Tortonese, E., *Osteichthyes (pesci ossei) Part 2. Fauna d'italia.* Calderini, Bolgna, 1975. (Detailed works on the Italian fish fauna, valuable for their meticulous descriptions and systematic notes on species)

Atlantic

Campbell, A. C., *The Hamlyn Guide to the Seashore and Shallow Seas of Britain and Europe*. Hamlyn, London, 1976. (Well illustrated and authoritative text on general marine life)

Muus, B. and Dahlstrom, P., *Collins Guide to the Sea Fishes of Britain and North-Western Europe*. Collins, London, 1974. (Reliable only for the North Sea fauna; well illustrated)

Wheeler, A., *The Fishes of The British Isles and North West Europe*. Macmillan, London, 1969. (Includes all fishes down to 500 fathoms)

Freshwater fishes

Cîhăr, J., *A Colour Guide to Familar Freshwater Fishes*. Octopus, London, 1976. (An excellent, well-illustrated simple account)

Ladiges, W. and Vogt, D., *Die Susswasserfische Europas*. P. Parey, Hamburg and Berlin, 1965. (A good general and complete treatment of the fauna)

Muss, B. J. and Dahlstrom, P., *Collins Guide to the Freshwater Fishes of Britain and Europe*. Collins, London, 1967. (A well-illustrated general account of European fishes)

Designers/Artists
Illustrations drawn by Sergio Rizzato together with the following: Mondadori: 50, 67a, 186, 188, 189, 194; Giorgio Arvati: 16, 17a; Giambattista Bertelli: 23, 26, 27, 30, 31, 34–35, 37a, 40L, 45, 47L, 63, 69, 76a, 107, 114, 115, 126–127; Luciano Corbella: 90, 91, 224; Piero Cozzaglio: 10a; Raffaele Curiel: 39; Gastone Rossini: 46, 152–153b; Raffaello Segattini: 17b, 36L, 37b, 42, 43, 47r, 48, 54a, 62, 68, 75a, 77, 93, 136, 138b, 142, 161, 172r, 173a, 174L, 182–183, 185, 200, 223b, 240a.

Photographs
G. Annunziata/Luisa Ricciarini: 104b, 120, 122; Mondadori: 10b, 11, 15, 41L, 57, 134, 198r, 239, 241, 244L, 245r; Chaumeton, Jacana: 81; Paolo Curto/Luisa Ricciarini: 209; R. Dei/Luisa Ricciarini: 38; Gillon, Jacana: 176; Vici, Jacana: 102b; J.-L. Lubrano, Parigi: 12, 13, 14; Maltini-Solaini/Luisa Ricciarini: 20bL, 157; Aldo Margiocco: 49, 89, 105b, 138a, 171a, 198L, 199 237; Marka Graphic: 244–245b; Giuseppe Mazza: 19b, 29, 41r, 72b, 80, 82a, 88b, 94, 100, 101, 102a, 117b, 118, 119, 123, 124, 129b, 130, 131, 132, 140, 144, 145, 150–151, 154, 155, 162, 163a, 164, 165, 166, 167, 168, 169b, 177, 202, 203, 207c/b, 208, 210, 211, 227a, 228–229b, 230, 231, 232, 233, 234, 235; P. Mongini: 227b; Lino Pellegrini: 225; Pictor, Milano: 20–21, 82–83b, 109, 160, 243; Folco Quilici: 222–223, 240b, 242, 244–245c; Enrico Robba/Luisa Ricciarini: 88a; R. Thompson/F. W. Lane: 137; G. Tomsich/Luisa Ricciarini: 106; Union Press: 18, 158–159, 190–191, 201, 204–205, 246–247; Visage, Jacana: 102c.

Index

255